DATE DUE

D1303880

Practi
for Ad

A Selectio
for Adult

by Anna Si

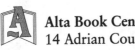

Alta Book Center Publishers
14 Adrian Court • Burlingame, California 94010 USA

Acquisitions Editor: Aaron Berman
Production Editor: Jamie Cross
Cover Art: Bruce Marion Design
Interior Design: Leigh McLellan Design
Title Script: Peter Linato

Alta Book Center Publishers

14 Adrian Court
Burlingame, California 94010 USA
PHONE: 800 ALTA/ESL • 650.692.1285—INT'L
FAX: 800 ALTA/FAX • 650.692.4654—INT'L
EMAIL: info@altaesl.com • WEBSITE: www.altaesl.com

ISBN 1-882483-80-4

Library of Congress Card Number: 00-100876

Acknowledgements

The authors would like to thank the following colleagues for their input, help and advice:

Sharron Bassano, Shirley Brod, Dana Cole, Paula Cosko, Jean Hanslin, Sandra Heyer, Susan Huss-Lederman, Jill Kramer, Heather McKay, Linda Mrowicki, Dawn Rammaha, Beth Rodacker-Borgens, Dianne E. Scott, Carolyn Tiller, Peggy Wahlen.

Thanks also to the many publishers and agencies that sent materials so that we could review them.

Dedication

*With thanks to all the ESL teachers and students who
have taught us so much, we dedicate this book to you.*

*And to everyone who reads this book:
May you take pride in the work you are doing.*

—Abbie & Anna

Contents

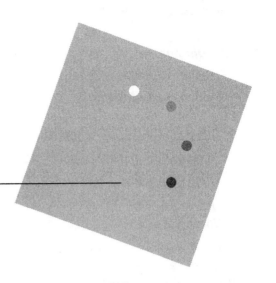

Introduction 1

1. Methods and Techniques 7

Basic Methods and
Techniques 8

Advanced Methods and
Techniques 10

Curriculum Planning 13

2. Coursebooks 15

3. Literacy 21

About Literacy Instruction 22

Student Materials 24

4. Teaching Activities 29

General Activities 30

Visuals 36

Games 39

Puzzles 41

Music 41

5. Speaking and Listening 43

Speaking/Conversation:

Teacher Resources 44
Student Materials 45

Listening:

Teacher Resources 50
Student Materials 51

Pronunciation:

Teacher Resources 56
Student Materials 57

6. Reading 61

Teacher Resources 62

Student Books:
Beginning Level 63

Student Books:
Intermediate Level 67

Student Books:
Advanced Level 70

Reading for Pleasure 72

7. Writing 75

Teacher Resources 76

Student Materials 78

8. Grammar   83

Teacher Resources 84

Student Materials 86

9. Dictionaries and Vocabulary   91

Picture Dictionaries 92

Text Dictionaries 94

Special Purpose Dictionaries . . 98

Vocabulary 99

Idioms 101

10. English for Specific Purposes   105

Survival Skills 106

Workplace and Work
   Readiness 108

Citizenship Test Preparation . 112

Civic Participation 116

11. Culture and Community Life   119

Culture and History 119

Holidays 123

Community Resources 124

12. Multi-Media Resources   127

TV and Video 127

Computer Skills and
   Computer Assisted Language
   Learning (CALL) 129

Internet ESL 130

Other Internet Resources 131

13. Publishers and Distributors   133

About Distributors 133

Publishers and Distributors . . 134

**Glossary:
A Shopper's Guide to Jargon**   147

Index   153

Introduction

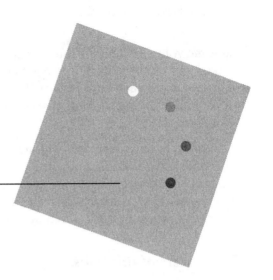

Help!! I've been given a beginners' class and I start on Monday!!" "I'm teaching a multilevel ESL class at a factory and I don't know where to start." "I'm a former elementary teacher and have never taught adults before." "I've taught advanced ESL for a long time but now I'm teaching literacy students." "I'm starting a citizenship class next week. Can you suggest any materials?"

These are just some of the cries for help we hear from colleagues, teachers we meet at workshops and meetings and, in Anna's case, from readers of *Hands-on English*. We wrote this book in order to answer some of these questions.

The authors

First, who are we? Between us we have about 45 years of ESL teaching experience with students from many different countries.

Abbie Tom: "I started out as a Spanish teacher but soon changed over to ESL. First I worked in the international office of a university, teaching ESL, working with volunteer tutors, advising students, and teaching ESL methods. Then I taught in an intensive program at a different university and I also taught ESL composition. Later I taught beginning students in one middle school and a multilevel class in another. Now I'm teaching in an adult program in Chapel Hill, North Carolina. I'm a volunteer tutor in a middle school. I also do teacher training for both volunteer and paid teachers and write teacher resource books."

Anna Silliman: "I trained as a German language teacher and first taught English overseas in adult programs, as well as in a university setting. In the U.S. I've taught ESL in a refugee program, in several different kinds of adult programs for immigrants, at a community college and in a university intensive English program. I also did some volunteer literacy tutoring and taught informal conversation classes. I've worked with students from very beginning through advanced levels, although much of my work has been with intermediate-level students. Currently I spend most of my time networking with other teachers for *Hands-on English* from my office in Crete, Nebraska."

Both of us have been around long enough that we've seen many teaching fashions come and go—some of them even recycled with new names. Practically speaking, no one approach works for everyone or for all students. So we've learned to combine the best of what's available and use a lot of different approaches to discover what works best for different students.

The readers of this book

Now, who are you? We have written this book for teachers and tutors of ESL to adults, ESL program administrators, literacy volunteer organizations and teacher trainers. We are thinking particularly of those who are new to the field or who are looking for specific resources to meet the needs of their students.

We recognize that those who teach ESL to adults work in a variety of settings. These might include adult basic skills programs in a school district or community college; prison education programs; church, synagogue or other programs affiliated with religious groups; workplace education programs; and library literacy programs or other volunteer tutoring programs. We know that adult ESL teachers and tutors contend with many difficulties and frustrations, from borrowed classrooms and lack of materials to multilevel classes, open enrollment and irregular attendance. Frequently teachers also find a lack of staff development opportunities and little program planning or support. They may also be isolated physically from other teachers doing similar work.

At the same time though, we know that teaching ESL to adults is exciting, fun and deeply rewarding, which more than compensates for the frustrations. Teachers who stick with this job know how important English skills are in the lives of their students, and they are dedicated to giving students the tools and skills they need.

The purpose of this book

How can this book help you? We know that materials appropriate for adults can sometimes be hard to find. In writing this book, we tried to think of all those questions teachers have asked us and then we looked for the most practical, useful books in the field which could help to answer them. We have written a brief description of each of our selections to help you decide if it has something you can use. In some cases, we have also added individual comments, preceded by our initials, AS and AT.

We hope that this bibliography will help you select books and materials that are truly useful in teaching ESL to adults. We have all had the experience of ordering a book that sounded wonderful and then finding it wasn't at all what we expected. Most of us, and our programs, don't have the time or money to waste in hunting for materials. We hope our notes will make your selections easier.

What's in this book

You can use this resource book in several ways. The book is organized into thirteen chapters; the first 12 are based on the main categories of materials that adult ESL teachers most often seek, and the final one lists contact information for publishers and distributors. We've included a glossary at the end of the book to help clarify some of the terms used in the descriptions. In addition, we have put together an index to help you identify materials by level, by content or by topics of special interest. We hope you find the book easy to navigate and fun to browse through.

Language levels

In some cases we have indicated what we believe to be the actual level of the material relative to adult programs, which is not always the same as what the publishers indicate. Publishers consider a variety of audiences, both foreign and domestic, from secondary school to pre-university and adult. The understanding of what constitutes "beginning," "intermediate" and "advanced" varies considerably from one setting to another.

In order to make our descriptions easier to interpret, we are providing here an explanation of what we mean when we refer to each of these levels in adult programs: literacy level, low-beginning, beginning, high-beginning, low-intermediate, intermediate, high-intermediate and advanced levels. (These last seven levels may correspond approximately to the seven Student Performance Levels, or SPL's, used in some programs.)

Literacy level

Many adult programs have literacy level students. Literacy students may not be literate in their first language or they may not have had previous exposure to Roman script. While they may already have some speaking skills in English, especially if they have lived in this country for a time, their lack of reading skills prevents them from participating in classes where reading skills are assumed. Their self-study options are also limited, as most learning materials are based on reading. These students may for reasons of previous schooling or age, for example, need a more gradual introduction to English, and they will need specific literacy instruction. Because this kind of instruction is fundamentally different from traditional second language instruction, we have dedicated a special section (Chapter 3) to materials for literacy students.

Beginning level

Beginners are usually considered to have some literacy skills already; that is, they can read and write in their own language. Low beginners, sometimes known as 'true beginners,' haven't had any introduction to English and may only know a few words, such as greetings. Most of their English language skills are at a zero level.

It's more usual, though, that beginning students have had at least some exposure to English, spoken or written, in school or in the workplace or through self-study, and they probably have some familiarity with the Roman alphabet. Their language skills may vary; for example some beginning students may speak with fluency (without much accuracy) but have limited experience reading and writing English. Others may have experience, for example in secondary school, with reading, writing and translating but have very limited functioning in listening and speaking. In general, though, beginning students' vocabulary is so limited that they will have great difficulty making themselves understood except in the context of the ESL class.

High beginners are able to read short passages edited for ESL, provided that they are in a familiar context and are presented with some support (previewing the title and accompanying pictures, for example). They can understand the teacher's simplified speech, and they can speak well enough to carry out communicative pair and small group activities in class, again with some preparation, but will have a hard time communicating with native speakers. They can write short passages with support, such as discussion and cue words, but not necessarily with accuracy. Their vocabulary is still restricted mostly to everyday needs.

Intermediate level

Low-intermediate students are still learning the basic structures of English. They are still limited to communicating in a controlled environment and reading mostly adapted material. However, they are writing and speaking with more complex sentences and vocabulary than beginners and starting to express their own ideas independently. Their vocabulary is expanding beyond the concrete and they can make at least some use of an all-English learner's dictionary.

Intermediate level speakers can usually find a way to make themselves understood, although with inaccuracies and hesitations in speech. With help from the teacher, they are just able to comprehend some unadapted material, such as newspapers or TV segments on certain topics. They are able to discuss familiar topics with native speakers, although with some paraphrasing. Intermediate students who have jobs are able to take verbal instruction from their employers without requiring visual demonstration or translation. They are able to use an all-English learner's dictionary effectively and their vocabulary is expanding rapidly. It is at this level that students start acquiring many more complex language structures.

High-intermediate students are starting to understand nearly everything in normal conversation with native speakers. Their speech may still be hesitant and not idiomatic, but they can express their ideas clearly and appropriately. They still make structural errors both in speaking and writing, but these do not interfere significantly with meaning. They still make frequent use of a dictionary, especially when reading material on an unfamiliar topic. Understanding TV and newspapers at this level is challenging, but possible, especially with some guidance.

Advanced level

In an adult program, advanced level students are not quite ready for academic work. Should they choose to apply to a college or university program, they may still be just before the point of preparing for the TOEFL exam. They probably have a lot of vocabulary and are just starting to learn to speak idiomatically. Their comprehension is good enough that they could take dictation from an unfamiliar text, for example, and can follow much of what they hear on TV; they can read a newspaper with some use of a dictionary. They can express their own ideas clearly and make good arguments, but they often need more practice in speaking. Frequently what students need at this level is to learn more idiomatic expressions, and if they have academic goals they also need to be reading extensively without the use of a dictionary, to continue expanding their vocabulary and their reading fluency. They should also be writing frequently. Note: Sometimes advanced learners refer themselves to adult programs because they have pronunciation problems they can't resolve elsewhere.

Mixed skill levels

Keep in mind that for most students, their various language skills will be at different levels, so that their grammar, reading and writing skills, for example, might be at an advanced level, but their speaking and listening is still at a low-intermediate level. This is frequently the case with students who studied English in their home country. Other students may become very fluent in speaking and communicating but come into a program with only beginning level reading and writing skills and little structure. Often students who have learned English on their own after arriving here fit this category. Every student differs in his or her own learning process. The goal for most students should be to bring their weaker skills up to par with their stronger skills, while still making progress overall.

How we made our selections

What criteria did we use in selecting the over 260 titles for this bibliography? First, we considered whether the materials are appropriate for adults. Are the topics relevant and interesting to adults? Do they speak to the needs of adults living in an English-speaking community? Do they take into account the life experiences and knowledge of adult students? Do they teach without patronizing? Do the illustrations and stories show adults rather than children? Do they use the students' time wisely? Do they challenge students to use English? Second, is the level of the material appropriate for the students who will be using it? Literacy books with busy pages and complex directions, for example, are overwhelming to many students. Third, does the content of the book match with current thinking about language teaching? Are students encouraged to use the language for real communication? Are the elements of language integrated, reading with writing with grammar with speaking, and so forth?

We didn't include those titles we looked at but felt were not useful. We also left out some wonderful books because they are unfortunately no longer in print. Some titles we just didn't get a chance to see and these could be included in a future edition.

As we write this, we are already thinking about next time, a second edition, with more books and reviews. We hope that you will help us with that effort by telling us which books you and your students like and use.

You can write to the authors of this book in care of the publisher, or you can contact us by email:

Anna Silliman, anna@handsonenglish.com
Abbie Tom, abtom@mindspring.com

Methods and Techniques

What teaching methods work best with adult ESL students? Books on ESL methods and techniques rarely address this question because they are generally written for a broader audience of teachers, including teachers in both domestic and foreign situations; teachers of children, adolescents, adults and university students; teachers of general courses and of specific courses like academic writing or English in the workplace.

For this chapter we have selected books on teaching methods which are of particular interest to teachers of adults. The first section, *Basic Methods and Techniques*, includes books for novice teachers which provide background information on the psychological, social, and linguistic basis of current language teaching. These selections also describe specific methods of teaching.

The second section, *Advanced Methods and Techniques*, is for teachers with some experience who want to dig deeper into others' ideas about teaching as they explore their own. Again we have selected books with particular relevance to teaching adults.

The third category, *Curriculum Planning*, is useful for program directors and planners as they organize or reorganize their programs.

For more specific "how-to" information, see our *Teacher's Resources* section in many of the other chapters.

Basic Methods and Techniques

#1-1

Approaches and Methods in Language Teaching: A Description and Analysis (1986) by Jack C. Richards and Theodore S. Rodgers. Cambridge: Cambridge University Press. 171pp. ISBN 0-521-31255-8.

This is a good, brief introduction to a variety of teaching approaches and methods, which the authors help the reader understand, evaluate and compare. They explain each one in terms of the underlying theory and its implementation (describing, for example, teacher and learner roles and procedures used in teaching). Each chapter has a lengthy bibliography for those who wish to learn more about a particular topic.

#1-2

The ESL Starter Kit (1998) by the Virginia Adult Education and Literacy Centers. Richmond: Virginia Commonwealth University. This 182-page book is available for reading online or downloading at http://www.vcu.edu/aelweb or free by mail from Virginia Adult Education and Literacy Centers, Virginia Commonwealth University, Oliver Hall Room 4080, 1015 West Main Street, PO Box 842020, Richmond, VA 23284-2020. Phone: 1-800-237-0178.

This is an excellent resource for those who are starting ESL programs of any kind. It has sections on registration and assessment, finding resources, planning lessons, managing multilevel classes, using effective teaching strategies and organizing a curriculum, to name only a few topics. In short, it includes everything you need to know to get started. Each section also includes resource lists for further study. The book is written in a very accessible and practical way.

#1-3

Making It Happen: Interaction in the Second Language Classroom: From Theory to Practice, Second Edition (1988, 1995) by Patricia A. Richard-Amato. New York: Addison Wesley Longman, now Pearson Education. 496pp. ISBN 0-201-42018-X.

This is a thorough introduction to interactive language teaching. Each chapter includes teaching activities and questions for reflection or discussion. There is a brief description of an adult program. The last section of the book has selected essays by important writers in the field, including two excellent ones on communicative language teaching and a useful one on personality factors and their relationship to language learning.

#1-4

Partnerships in Learning: Teaching ESL to Adults (1996) by Julia Robinson and Mary Selman. Toronto: Pippin Publishing. This title is one in their *Teachers' Library* series. 128pp. ISBN 0-88751-074-4.

This highly readable book begins with a description of adult language learners and proceeds to tell the reader everything he or she needs to know about teaching them, from assessing needs to planning lessons. It's an excellent starting place for a new teacher.

#1-5

Teaching Adult Second Language Learners (1999) by Heather McKay and Abigail Tom. New York: Cambridge University Press. 200pp. ISBN 0-521-64990-0.

The first section of this book provides basic information about teaching second languages to adults: who the students are, how to assess them, how to organize a curriculum and how to plan a lesson. The remainder of the book has easy-to-use activities organized thematically. In one activity in the health section, for example, students consider various solutions to first aid problems; in another they learn to do the Heimlich maneuver. Themes include community building, family, housing, money, health and food.

#1-6

Teaching Adults: An ESL Resource Book (1996) developed by Laubach Literacy Action. Syracuse: New Readers Press. 175pp. ISBN 1-56420-130-9. *(If you order this, make sure they send you the ESL book; there is a literacy book with almost the same title.)*

This book is written for volunteer tutors but is also useful for beginning teachers, as it gives a clear introduction to many kinds of ESL teaching activities. For example, the book includes a description of TPR (Total Physical Response) lessons, shows you how to generate a Language Experience story with a student (and how to use such stories for skill-building), and gives many examples of information-gap activities. These are presented in a detailed, step-by-step manner that is accessible to any thoughtful reader. There is also good advice here on how to understand the process of language learning.

#1-7

Teaching by Principles: An Interactive Approach to Language Pedagogy (1994) by H. Douglas Brown. Upper Saddle River: Prentice Hall Regents, now Pearson Education. 467pp. ISBN 0-13-328220-1. (A new edition is forthcoming.)

This basic methods book is based on twelve cognitive, affective, and linguistic principles teachers may use to guide their classroom choices. After reviewing past approaches to language teaching, the author describes today's communicative language teaching as an informed and eclectic approach. The book includes clear definitions of commonly used terms, such as cooperative learning and whole language. It has an excellent section contrasting teaching children and adults (especially useful for those who come to adult teaching from elementary schools) and a good section on learner strategy training. The author explains specific ways of teaching communicatively. The main drawback of this book is its length.

#1-8

Teaching English as a Second or Foreign Language, Second Edition (1991) Marianne Celce-Murcia, editor. Boston: Heinle & Heinle Publishers. 567pp. ISBN 0-8384-2860-6.

This is a general methods textbook, with articles on many aspects of language teaching. There are two chapters specifically about teaching adults. One is a helpful article on literacy by Wayne Haverson describing differing approaches to teaching reading and what is involved in learning to read. It provides practical suggestions for teaching literacy students. The second, an article by Sharon Hilles, provides a 12-page overview of teaching adult ESL students, placed in the larger context of adult education. Also, an important article on experiential language learning by Janet Eyring introduces the concept of an integrated approach, with some good examples. Finally, the two chapters on teaching listening are excellent, providing both theory and specific suggestions for teaching. AS: "The literacy article would be a good place to start for someone brand new to the field."

#1-9

Teaching Multilevel Classes in ESL (1991) by Jill Bell. San Diego: Dominie Press, Inc. 165pp. ISBN 1-56270-032-4.

This very friendly and accessible book begins by describing a typical multilevel adult ESL class and its students and then leads the teacher through planning, assessment, management and activities for such a class. The author's key concept for teaching a multilevel class is to organize it around one theme (health, for example) and to provide activities for students at different levels within this theme. She illustrates this well with detailed examples from real classrooms. Once you get this key concept, the impossible is doable. AT: "It is extremely useful as well as comforting (you are not alone!)."

Advanced Methods and Techniques

#1-10

Caring and Sharing in the Foreign Language Classroom: A Sourcebook on Humanistic Techniques (1978) by Gertrude Moskowitz. Boston: Heinle & Heinle Publishers. 343pp. ISBN 0-8384-2771-5.

This is a classic work on humanistic language teaching. The author first describes what she means by humanistic teaching, which to her is much more than just personalizing your lessons; it includes making the person part of the content of the course. While some of the language about feelings may sound dated, the principles she espouses are still valid. She provides a wealth of classroom activities, many of which are still interesting. This is a good source for activities that make use of visualizing skills and that affirm the value of the individual.

#1-11
Community Spirit: A Practical Guide to Collaborative Language Learning (1995)
by Sharron Bassano and Mary Ann Christison. San Francisco: Alta Book Center
Publishers. 124pp. ISBN 1-882483-30-8.

This book provides specific suggestions and encouragement to the teacher
who wants to have a student-centered, collaborative classroom. The ideas are
clearly presented and the concrete suggestions are teacher-tested. Just one example: To encourage peer tutoring, first teach an item to four students, then
have each of them teach it to another student and so on until all the students
have learned it. Then all students meet together to test what they've learned.
The book includes interactive strategies for all levels, arranged by type (such
as matching, sequencing, classifying, and charts and grids). The strategies can
easily be adapted for any class. AS: "This is an especially user-friendly book."

#1-12
Designing Tasks for the Communicative Classroom (1989) by David Nunan. Victoria: Cambridge University Press. 209pp. 0-521-37915-6.

This is not a book for the novice teacher, but is an interesting and provocative one for the experienced. It provides a sophisticated analysis of communicative language teaching and language skills and explores the kinds of tasks
which suit this view of teaching and learning.

#1-13
Mistakes and Correction (1989) by Julian Edge. New York: Longman, now Pearson Education. 70pp. ISBN 0-582-74626-4.

Although the topic of the book is rather specific, what to do about mistakes
and correction is an issue of concern to many language teachers. The author
discusses kinds of mistakes and their relative importance. He makes suggestions
about how to correct errors when it is appropriate.

#1-14
Principles and Practice in Second Language Acquisition (1982, 1988) by Stephen
D. Krashen. New York: Prentice Hall, now Pearson Education. 202pp. ISBN 0-13-
710047-7.

This book focuses on Krashen's theories of language learning. It is a good
source for learning more about these ideas, which have had a major impact
on how teachers view the process of language learning.

#1-15
Reflective Teaching in Second Language Classrooms (1994) by Jack C. Richards
and Charles Lockhart. Cambridge: Cambridge University Press. 256pp. ISBN 0-
521-45803-X.

This is a useful tool for teachers to examine their own work or as a basis
for inservice teacher training. While not specifically intended for teachers of
adults, it is adaptable to any teaching situation.

#1-16

Roles of Teachers and Learners (1987) by Tony Wright. Oxford: Oxford University Press. 164pp. ISBN 0-19-437133-6.

This thought-provoking book explores the factors which influence the roles of teachers and students. It leads the reader to consider his or her attitudes toward teaching and learning through a consideration of actual situations and tasks.

#1-17

Self-Access (1989) by Susan Sheerin. Oxford: Oxford University Press. 200pp. ISBN 0-19-437099-2. (This book has now gone out of print but may still be found in libraries or resource centers.)

This is one of the few books available to those who want to set up centers for "do it yourself" learning within their classes. It provides useful "how to" information as well as specific activities which can be adapted to different levels and kinds of students. Teachers of large multilevel classes may find this a useful way for portions of the class to work productively on their own while the teacher works with small groups.

#1-18

The Self-Directed Teacher: Managing the Learning Process (1996) by David Nunan and Clarice Lamb. Cambridge: Cambridge University Press. 296pp. ISBN 0-521-49773-6.

This is a very thoughtful and thought-provoking book about the decisions teachers must make as they teach. It includes reflective tasks which can be used by a group of teachers doing training together or by individual readers.

#1-19

Testing for Language Teachers (1989) by Arthur Hughes. Cambridge: Cambridge University Press. 172pp. ISBN 0-521-27260-2.

As demands for accountability increase in adult programs, the issue of testing has become more important. Although this is a serious book on a complex topic, the author has managed to present the information in a way that is not intimidating to the reader. He gives very specific instructions on how to make effective tests, taking the reader step-by-step through the process of making various kinds of tests and test items.

#1-20

Working with Teaching Methods: What's at Stake? (1998) by Earl W. Stevick. Pacific Grove: Heinle & Heinle Publishers. 192pp. ISBN 0-8384-7891-3.

This is a re-working of Stevick's classic *Teaching Languages: A Way and Ways,* and like his other books is well worth reading and thinking about. It is not a book that tells you what to do tomorrow. Instead, it carries the reader with the author as he examines what he has learned about language teaching. In it he takes a very personal look at various approaches to language learning.

The book is very nicely laid out, with marginal notes, theoretical frameworks, case studies and suggestions for further investigation. More than any other writer in our field, Stevick will get you to think about the meaning of teaching and learning.

#1-21
Techniques for Classroom Interaction (1987) by Donn Byrne. New York: Longman, now Pearson Education. 108pp. ISBN 0-582-74627-2.

This is a very accessible, even chatty, book which encourages teachers to consider alternative ways of teaching by increasing the use of interactive activities. The author raises objections teachers might have to such activities and responds to them with specific activities.

#1-22
Testing Spoken Language: A Handbook of Oral Testing Techniques (1987) by Nic Underhill. Cambridge: Cambridge University Press. 128pp. ISBN 0-521-31276-0.

This is a useful book for teachers and administrators considering how best to test students' oral skills. It contains everything one needs to know about the topic, including types of oral tests, their pros and cons and ways to administer them.

Curriculum Planning

#1-23
The Learner-Centered Curriculum: A Study in Second Language Teaching (1988) by David Nunan. Victoria: Cambridge University Press. 208pp. ISBN 0-521-35843-4.

This thought-provoking book is useful for directing and expanding the thinking of those engaged in curriculum planning. Unlike many books on curriculum planning, it focuses on adult classes and programs and the particular needs of adult learners. It brings together research on this topic from many different sources. While it is not easy reading, the book is well-organized so that the reader can find those topics of special interest. The book also contains excellent charts showing, for example, the characteristics of traditional and communicative teaching, factors in judging task difficulty and key questions in evaluation.

#1-24
Making Meaning, Making Change: Participatory Curriculum Development for Adult ESL Literacy (1992) by Elsa Roberts Auerbach. McHenry: Delta Systems/ Center for Applied Linguistics. 140pp. ISBN 0-93-735479-1.

This book describes a participatory approach to curriculum development used in a specific project in Massachusetts. At the same time it engages the reader in a step-by-step consideration of his or her own program's curriculum.

There is a lot of good information, for example, on ways to create student-centered materials. The book includes a good section on alternative forms of evaluation. It is a very useful tool for staff development. (See also *Talking Shop*, below.)

#1-25

Talking Shop: A Curriculum Sourcebook for Participatory Adult ESL (1992) by Andrea Nash, Ann Cason, Madeline Rhum, Loren McGrail, Rosario Gomez-Sanford. McHenry: Delta Systems/Center for Applied Linguistics. 70pp. ISBN 0-93-735478-3.

This is a companion book to *Making Meaning, Making Change* (item #1-24 above). In this highly readable book, five teachers describe their experiences with participatory learning. They describe their classes and specific lessons. It is a very personal book, reflecting the authors' thoughts about teaching. It's rather like sitting in a teacher's room after class and talking about what you've been doing. It is of more interest to experienced teachers than to novices.

See also:
NCLE (item #13-24 in the *Publishers* section) for short articles on curriculum guidelines and on techniques for teaching adult ESL.

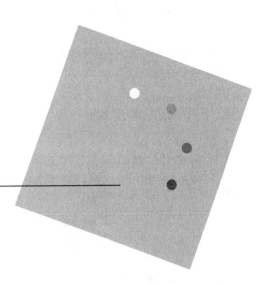

Coursebooks

Most of the books and series we've selected for this chapter provide a complete language course, integrating listening, speaking, grammar, reading, writing and vocabulary. Some of them also provide important lifeskills or cultural information. In many cases there are supplementary materials for the teacher, such as tapes, computer software, overheads, pictures or charts. Typically there is a set format for each unit within a coursebook. In some cases there are continuing characters or stories throughout the text. Usually coursebook materials are intended to form a coherent and ongoing structure for classroom work.

Pros and cons

Having all of this material available, "ready made," is especially useful for a beginning teacher because he or she does not have to begin from scratch preparing materials. Decisions about when and how to present certain structures have already been made by the author. Other advantages of using a coursebook are that it is easier to establish a routine in the class, there is more security for both the students and the teacher because there is a plan, and there is continuity from lesson to lesson, as well as within a program where a series of books is used.

The disadvantage of adopting a coursebook is that the text can become too predictable and therefore boring, and also that no one coursebook is entirely suitable for all students. Many experienced teachers therefore prefer teaching without such coursebooks because it allows them more flexibility to meet the needs of their students. If they do use a coursebook, they usually supplement it with many other materials to keep things interesting and relevant to the students (see, for example, books listed under *Activities* in Chapter 4), or with further structure exercises (see *Grammar*, Chapter 8). Additional reading materials are usually needed as well, since most coursebooks offer limited opportunities for reading extended text (see *Reading*, Chapter 6).

Communication is key

The books we have selected for this section reflect our belief that language teaching should begin with communication, and with real language as it is used in authentic contexts. All of these books will provide you with examples of real language as a place to start.

Note: Coursebooks intended for literacy level students are listed separately in the *Literacy* section, Chapter 3.

Coursebooks

#2-1

Collaborations: English in Our Lives Beginning Book 1 (1996) by Gail Weinstein-Shr and Jann Huizenga (and others). Boston: Heinle & Heinle Publishers. Beginning Book 1 is 112pp, ISBN 0-8384-4106-8. Beginning Book 2, Intermediate Books 1 & 2 and Literacy level are also available. A teacher's edition, activity masters, maps, transparencies, audio cassette tape, a teacher's resource kit and an assessment package are available for each level.

This is a five-level series, going from literacy through the intermediate level. The content revolves around real adult ESL students in North America, their lives and the places they live and work. For example, in a unit on work, immigrant Gloria Sierra tells about her job as a school bus driver in Bernanillo, New Mexico. Two kinds of dictation give students practice with this story; they then describe and compare other jobs, both orally and in writing. There follows an interview activity in which students talk with their classmates about each other's work. Then students read several short stories about other people's jobs, which are likely to raise issues they are interested in discussing.

The workbook provides more extensive writing practice, practice with the new vocabulary and grammar exercises. The teacher's book provides author's notes about implementing the activities including some explanation about the intended objectives. We were interested in the field testers' notes, which tell you how other teachers and their students reacted to each activity.

The series provides plenty of opportunities for students to discuss their own experiences, and to interact and practice English. Cultural information is integrated into the content. At the end of each unit is a learning log where students can check what they have learned. It is a well-organized and well-presented series. It is most suited to students who are already engaged in their life in the U.S. but who are perhaps still struggling with issues of cultural differences. AT: "I like the variety of age and ethnicity in the photographs."

#2-2

Conversations in English, (Book 2 in the Basic ESL Series, 1995) by Linda Mrowicki and Janet Isserlis. Palatine: Linmore Publishing. 132pp. ISBN 0-916591-33-3. A teacher's book, an audio cassette tape and a very complete teacher resource book, which provides reproducible activities as well as guidance in using the book, are also available.

This is the second book in the Linmore Basic ESL Series (see the *Literacy* section for *First Words,* #3-12), and is appropriate for low beginners. There are 14 units on topics such as introductions, "How was your weekend?" and where students go shopping. Each unit begins with a picture, followed by guided conversation, interviews and student stories. Students are given plenty of opportunities for reading and writing as well as speaking and listening.

The photographs and drawings used to enhance meaning are very clear. For example, in Lesson 7 about free time, students brainstorm a list of sports activities. They look at photos of sports and hobby equipment and identify which sport or hobby goes with each. Then they read and practice a conversation about free time, and practice this with a partner. Using a chart, students gather information about each others' sports interests and discuss the results with the class. They read three stories about people and their interests, and answer some questions. Finally, based on some questions, they write a paragraph about how they spend their own free time.

We like the realistic, personal nature of this material. The book is easy to implement in class and it will encourage even timid students to participate and use new structures successfully. All of the materials are reasonably priced.

#2-3

Crossroads (1991) Book 1 by Irene Frankel and Cliff Meyers (Books 2, 3 and 4 are also available). New York: Oxford University Press. Student Book 1 is 130pp., ISBN 0-19-434376-6. For each level, a teacher's book, audio cassette tapes, workbook and a 'multilevel activity and resources package' (MARP) are also available. Achievement and placement tests are offered separately.

This is a carefully thought out series with authentic language and situations for adults. It starts at a lower level of English than most other coursebooks and it moves forward at a slower pace than other series, giving students plenty of opportunities to recycle the language structures and really master them. The exercises in every chapter provide low-stress listening practice and information-gap pairwork activities that help students practice what they've learned. There is a variety of types of reading, including conversations, forms and maps. Short writing exercises accompany each section in the chapter.

The content of this series incorporates both the basic structures of the language and some of the real-life situations students may encounter. For example, Unit 4 in Book 1, *Community Services,* is about reporting an emergency—it starts with a drawing of two men spotting smoke coming out of a building and running to a pay phone. The students hear a dialogue about calling the fire department, then they read this and practice it. Next they extend this to calling an ambulance and the police; they practice giving an address, as well as numbers and ordinal numbers (i.e., seventh floor). The chapter concludes with map activities (i.e., "it's on the corner of Sixth Street and Washington Avenue") which they can work on in pairs.

The valuable resource packet that comes with each level provides the teacher with grammar exercises (reproducible worksheets) at two different levels, more pairwork for student practice, picture stories and a game for language practice— for every chapter! We love the life-sized face pictures of the cast of characters in the book, which students can hold up and use for role-plays. Like many other aspects of the book, this is fun but not child-like in the least. The teacher's book is well worth studying, as it describes some teaching techniques that work well with beginning students, as well as giving step-by-step tips for each unit. The student books are relatively inexpensive; a good thing if you have a large program.

You might select this series for students who have relatively little education or experience in learning languages. It is best for those, like some refugee students, who are starting at zero level and really need to learn the basics and become functional in basic English as soon as possible.

See also:

Connect with English and *Crossroads Café* (items #12-2 and #12-3 in the *Video* section), two video series for classroom or self study, best for intermediate or advanced students.

English ASAP (item #10-5 in the *Workplace* section). This series provides a solid course in language skills in a workplace context.

English at Home and on the Road (item #11-4 in the *Culture* section), an all-skills text based on short cultural readings.

#2-4
LifePrints: ESL for Adults Books 1, 2 and 3 (1993) by Christy M. Newman with Allene Guss Grognet and JoAnn (Jodi) Crandall. Syracuse: New Readers Press. Book 1 is 128pp., ISBN 0-88336-034-9. For each level, an audio cassette tape, teacher's edition, assessment tests and a teacher's resource file with reproducible materials are also available.

This well-conceived series is clearly written for adults, using high-interest situations and language relevant to new arrivals. The book is organized by survival topics including: shopping, getting a driver's license and going to the doctor. These are familiar topics for beginning ESL texts, but in this series they are presented more seriously and in greater detail, with the aim of giving the students information they need to participate and make decisions. Language structures are introduced only as they are needed in context. The many illustrations are detailed and expressive, which is especially useful for literacy level students.

Each chapter is thorough and detailed. For example, the unit on driving a car (Book 2, Chapter 4) begins with a discussion of getting a driver's license. Students talk about their own experiences with driving. The next sections (applying for a permit, getting car insurance) each have a taped conversation which students listen to in order to learn important information such as what to take along to the DMV. The students take notes of this information. Next students read and practice information about road signs and parking from a driver's manual, and practice filling out an application for a license. In the following exercise, students hear an audiotape of a road test while looking at a map of the area and tracing the route. Finally, there is a section on being pulled over by the police, and students study and discuss an example of a speeding ticket. The last section describes a minor accident; the students talk about possible solutions to a problem.

Included in the resource file for the above chapter are seven handouts with detailed instructions which you could use to follow up or expand on the topic of driving. Also, the teacher's edition has suggestions for roleplays, discussion ideas and other follow-up activities. The explanations are detailed enough for new teachers to use successfully. There are few structure exercises.

You might select this text for new immigrant students who need to understand how things work in this country in order to be full participants. New arrivals at all levels will find the topics relevant. Unlike most adult series, it assumes that the student will continue through the program, so themes are not recycled at different levels.

#2-5
Real-Life English: A Competency-Based ESL Program for Adults **Books 1, 2, 3, 4 and Literacy level (1994). Austin: Steck-Vaughn Co. For each level, a workbook, teacher's edition and audio cassette tapes are also available. Book 1 is 158pp, ISBN 0-8114-3212-2.**

In addition to the literacy level text, this series includes four levels from low-beginning through intermediate. It covers the same survival topics (health care, shopping, transportation, etc.) in each level, so that the series could be used in a multilevel class. Each unit presents new material in the form of dialogues, which students listen to or read. For example, Unit 2 (*Our Community*) includes a telephone conversation in which a customer calls the gas company to report a gas leak. Several listening activities give students practice taking phone messages. Then students read a telephone bill and look for a mistake in the bill. Other community services are discussed in relation to the phone book 'blue pages.' Some structure exercises are included, and the workbook provides short exercises very similar to the material in the student book. The teacher's guide provides some good suggestions for relating the material to the students' own lives.

Throughout, the material is clear and straightforward enough that students could work on it independently. There is more listening and reading in the exercises than speaking and writing; fewer communicative activities than in some other books. This might be a text to select for relatively new arrivals who need to know, for example, how to call a poison control center and other basic life-skills matters. It may not be challenging enough to provide a strong language foundation though, so it would need to be supplemented with other materials.

#2-6

Short Cuts: An Interactive English Course, Books 1, 2, and 3 (1996) by James Mentel. New York: McGraw-Hill. Book 1 is 158pp. ISBN 0-07-041886-1. An instructor's manual, audio cassette tapes, transparencies and posters are available for each level.

The special feature of this book is the manipulatives, which appear in the back of the student book. Students remove the large picture from the back of the book and cut out the small pieces around the edges. They then use these to respond to aural and written material by moving the small pictures around on the page. The artwork is attractive and the concept of having students respond in this low-stress manner is appealing.

Each chapter in the book is based on a situation (school, kitchen, neighborhood, describing people, etc.) and is introduced with a large picture for students to discuss as they learn the new vocabulary. This is followed by a listening activity (for example, two students describing their teacher) and some group work for students to practice the new structures, using the manipulatives (this part could be fun if the students get into it). A short reading passage reviews the same content (for example, a letter from a student describing his teachers) and a structured writing activity has students try it themselves (for example, describe three people). There are four such cycles in each chapter. At the end of each chapter is a bit of grammar and some review exercises.

The material in this book is very structured and somewhat limited in the kind of vocabulary it presents. All of the situations are straightforward—there is no attempt to present dilemmas or problems to the students. There is also little challenge to the students to produce language independently. These features might be a plus for students who are fearful or intimidated about learning the language—sometimes elderly students appreciate this kind of approach, for example.

Book 1 could be used with real beginners who have some literacy but it is still too high for literacy students. Level 3 goes to about a high beginning level. Cassettes, transparencies and poster versions of the manipulatives are all available, as well as a teacher's manual. You'll definitely want the teacher's manual if you teach from this series—it gives ideas on how to make good use of the manipulatives. Because of all the little parts, the series may be a bit fussy for classes which meet in borrowed spaces. It might also prove confusing for students who do not attend classes regularly and for those who don't keep good track of their materials.

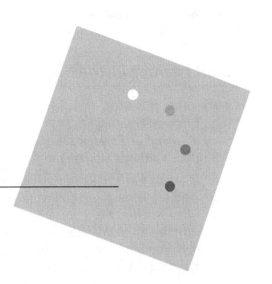

Literacy

Literacy-level instruction means teaching English to students who are not yet able to read and write in English. Some of these students may have had little or no schooling in their home countries. Others may have attended school, but learned to read a non-Roman alphabet. Special materials, techniques and approaches are required for these students. For this reason, we have chosen to provide a separate section on literacy.

A great challenge

Adult ESL literacy instruction may be the most difficult kind of ESL teaching. It is intense and exhausting and requires expertise different from other kinds of language teaching. Unfortunately, literacy classes are often assigned to novice teachers or combined with higher level classes. For those teachers new to literacy, we especially recommend *A Handbook for ESL Literacy* (item #3-7 below) as a starting point.

What's needed

Selecting appropriate materials for the students is essential. The student books we have included here reflect an approach that begins with the communication of meaning, with reading growing out of that meaning. Books for the beginning reader should integrate listening and speaking with reading and writing. They should have large, easy-to-read print and uncluttered pages. Directions should be clear and consistent. The content should be interesting and relevant to adult students. Illustrations should assist with meaning.

About Literacy Instruction

#3-1

"Adult Literacy Training" (1991) article by Wayne W. Haverson in *Teaching English as a Second or Foreign Language*, Marianne Celce Murcia, editor. (See item #1-8 in the Methods chapter).

This 10-page article describes possible approaches to teaching adult literacy and argues that a strategy-based model designed to promote learner success is most effective. The author advocates the active involvement of learners in activities linked to their lives and experiences. He describes characteristics of a beginning learner, how to select materials and ways to carry out instruction, with quite a few good teaching suggestions.

#3-2

Agendas for Second Language Literacy (1993) by Sandra L. McKay. Cambridge: Cambridge University Press. 151pp. ISBN 0-521-44664-3.

This book will help those teachers who wish to delve more deeply into literacy issues. The author considers what literacy means to individuals, families and society and what kinds of literacy are expected by different parts of society. This book does not, nor does it intend to, provide practical advice on how to teach literacy students.

#3-3

Approaches to Adult ESL Literacy Instruction (1993) by JoAnn Crandall and Joy Kreeft Peyton, editors. McHenry, IL: Delta Systems/Center for Applied Linguistics. 98pp. ISBN 0-93-7354-82-1.

This book contains essays on five current approaches in literacy instruction for adults: competency-based, whole language, language experience, learner-generated writing, and participatory education. These are described as starting points for instruction; the use of one does not exclude the others. While based in theory, each essay is well grounded in reality, with many specific examples and a bibliography for further information.

Chapter 3, *The Language Experience Approach* by Marcia L. Taylor, is an exceptionally clear and useful description of this technique and includes several good ways to use it in the classroom. We'd recommend this chapter to any teacher who would like to learn about the technique and why it works.

#3-4

Basic Oxford Picture Dictionary Literacy Program (1996) by Garnet Templin-Imel with Shirley Brod. New York: Oxford University Press. 283pp. ISBN 0-19-434573-4.

Designed for use with the *Basic Oxford Picture Dictionary* (item #9-1), this resource is a looseleaf binder full of materials for literacy teachers including reproducible student pages, teacher's notes, activities and tests. It provides a complete, four-skills language program integrated with life-skills activities. The first part includes general activities; the second part has specific activities that correspond to pages in the *Basic Oxford Picture Dictionary*. The directions for activities are very clear and complete (for that reason they may seem a little long). The initial cost may seem high, but it is an excellent resource and worth every penny.

#3-5
Beginners (1994) by Peter Grundy. Oxford: Oxford University Press. 149pp. ISBN 0-19-437200-6.

This is an excellent book about teaching beginners. The author introduces the book by describing the characteristics of different kinds of beginners. This is followed by a chapter on the decisions the teacher must make in teaching them. Each subsequent chapter has a very chatty and helpful introduction and contains interesting and useful activities. The author includes sections on such topics as using the Roman alphabet and using numbers. It is clear that he has worked with true beginners. AT: "This is a must for anyone teaching beginners."

#3-6
Bringing Literacy to Life: Issues and Options in Adult ESL Literacy (1992) by Heide Spruck Wrigley and Gloria J. A. Guth. San Diego: Dominie Press. 300pp. ISBN 1-56270-300-5.

This is a very rich book, with a great deal of practical advice as well as theory. It is not a book that will tell you what to do tomorrow, but it is one to which the thoughtful teacher will return again and again. Under each topic (including literacy, assessment, computer and video technology, and curriculum planning) are sub-sections on theory, practice and questions to ask about one's own program. For the classroom teacher, the most useful section may be Chapter 9, curriculum modules (or teaching units) by ten experienced ESL teachers. These provide many ideas to incorporate into your own teaching. For program directors, the book is a useful aid for program planning and staff development.

See also:
Chalk Talks (item #5-1 in the *Conversation* section) for a useful technique of recording students' stories in simple pictures, which can then be supplemented with writing.

#3-7
A Handbook for ESL Literacy (1984) by Jill Bell and Barbara Burnaby. Toronto: Ontario Institute for Studies in Education/Hodder & Stoughton Ltd (available from Pippin Publishing and book distributors). 140pp. ISBN 0-7744-0270-9.

This very readable book presents theoretical concerns in teaching ESL to adults, particularly those with literacy issues, as well as useful examples and specific activities for such classes. Chapter 10 gives more than twenty supplementary activities that help literacy students practice their new skills. Although the focus is on literacy, it is also an important book for anyone teaching ESL to adults. AT: "This is an excellent starting place for new teachers."

See also:
Keystrokes to Literacy (item #12-5 in the *Computer* section) for some step-by-step computer lessons your students might enjoy.

#3-8

"What Non-Readers or Beginning Readers Need to Know: Performance-Based ESL Adult Literacy" (1999) article by Shirley Brod. Denver: ELT Technical Assistance Project. 34pp. Published as a monograph.

This article presents a clear description of the needs and challenges of non-literate learners, and presents four important principles for helping these students succeed. Many specific guidelines and examples give you ways to implement these in the classroom. Rationale for performance-based instruction is given as well. We like the appendices, which give you in three pages the most important items students need to know how to read. It is well researched, with plenty of references.

Student Materials

See also:
Book One (item #5-24 in the *Listening* section), which gives a lot of low-stress reinforcement practice suitable for literacy-level students.

#3-9

Collaborations, English in Our Lives (1996), Literacy level by Donna Moss, Cathy C. Shank and Lynda Terrill. Boston: Heinle & Heinle Publishers. Literacy worktext is 156pp. ISBN 0-8384-6624-9. A teacher's edition, activity masters, transparencies, audio cassette tape, a teacher's resource kit and an assessment package are also available. (See item #2-1 in the *Coursebooks* section for details on the other levels.)

This book is intended for adults who need basic literacy skills such as reading and writing numbers, letters of the alphabet, dates, time and money. It is correlated to the higher levels in this series and so could be used in a multi-level setting. The unique feature of the book is that even at this very basic level of English, the lessons are based on stories about real students. For example, in a chapter about family members, a Cambodian man reminisces about his grandparents' farm. There is a wide variety of short activities that give students a chance to talk about themselves, interview other students, read about other students and even interview the teacher. Each exercise has a short reading and writing component as well as listening and speaking, so there is plenty of reinforcement. (The teacher's materials provide even more activities.)

The photographs and line drawings are plentiful and are mostly about people. This makes all the exercises quite concrete as well as interesting. We especially like the picture stories, which are usually about a person's day or part of a person's life. At the back of the book are some useful practice worksheets, including some nice ones on learning to read a calendar.

This book is useful for very beginning level students who have little or no literacy skills. Unlike many texts for such students, this one won't patronize them or make them feel stupid. It should give them a positive start in learning English language skills.

See also:

Crossroads, (item #2-3 in the *Coursebooks* section), a series that can be used with literacy level students (although it provides limited help for true literacy students) and has a multilevel component.

Easy True Stories (item #6-6 in the *Reading* section) for picture-based stories that can be adapted to literacy level students.

#3-10

English ASAP™: Connecting English to the Workplace, Literacy level (1999). Austin: Steck-Vaughn. 134pp. ISBN 0-8172-7950-4. A teacher's edition (including additional worksheets to practice literacy skills) and audio cassette tapes are available. (See item #10-5 in the *Workplace* section for the other levels in this series.)

This is a systematic textbook which uses workplace language as its core. Each short unit includes a clear picture to set the scene, for example a man cashing his paycheck at the bank, or a person refilling a copy machine. This is followed by a short dialogue (3 to 5 sentences) to introduce the language lesson. Some listening and some limited writing exercises follow each dialogue. The language that has been selected is applicable to most work situations and is suitable even for very beginning language learners. The book integrates all skills (reading, writing, listening, speaking) but does not provide any connected discourse for reading. Because each unit is short and limited to just a few language items, this material might work well in a class where regular attendance is a problem. The pictures are nice and help to provide more interest and depth (and discussion material) to an otherwise very basic text.

#3-11

First Class Reader! Integrated Skills Lessons for Beginners (1990, 1994) by Sharron Bassano with John Duffy. San Francisco: Alta Book Center Publishers. 129pp. ISBN 1-882483-29-4.

This book provides a systematic approach to literacy, beginning with pictures and individual words presented orally. Each of the 30 units is based on a story about students going about their daily lives. The text integrates listening, speaking and writing with reading in a consistent and clear format. Students are active participants in the process. The instructions to the teacher are clear and complete. This would be a good choice for a novice teaching a literacy-level class.

Since this book is very inexpensive, your program should be able to get class sets at a reasonable cost. This is an excellent, classroom-ready book.

#3-12
First Words in English (1990) by Linda Mrowicki. Palatine: Linmore Publishing. 125pp. ISBN 0-916591-21-2. A teacher's manual, teacher resource book and audio cassette tape are also available.

This is a very systematic and easy-to-use book for beginning readers, teaching basic survival, oral and literacy skills. It is organized around life-skill topics such as school, health and consumer education. Students begin each lesson by talking about photographs and then read and write related words and sentences. They also write information about themselves. In addition to the student book, there is a very thorough teacher's manual, which provides every bit of information a novice or volunteer tutor needs to get started. And, there is also an excellent teacher resource book, which contains additional reproducible activities and worksheets. The book and an accompanying cassette are very reasonably priced. See the *Coursebooks* section for another book in Linmore's Basic ESL series, *Conversations in English* (item #2-2).

See also:
LifePrints, a series from New Readers Press (item #2-4 in the *Coursebooks* section), which has detailed illustrations making it accessible to literacy-level students.

#3-13
Longman ESL Literacy, Second Edition (1991, 1998) by Yvonne Wong Nishio. White Plains: Addison Wesley Longman, now Pearson Education. Student book is 192pp. ISBN 0-201-35182-X. A teacher's resource book is also available.

This is a well-organized book for the beginning literacy student. It is organized around life-skill competencies such as telling time, counting money, making a phone call, buying something at the store and asking for directions. Students take an active role, using TPR (Total Physical Response), telling about their own lives, completing surveys of their classmates and participating in other activities. Each unit includes practice in all four language skills. The illustrations are very clear and written instructions are minimal, making the student book uncluttered and very accessible to students.

The Teacher's Resource Book, although somewhat expensive, is a necessary part of the program and is well worth buying. It provides excellent step-by-step guidance for a novice teacher or tutor as well as reproducible picture flashcards for each unit. The new edition of the teacher book has added short student readings, some with their own pictures and others corresponding to pictures in another section of the teacher book. The unit tests have a useful feature—the students answer by filling in an oval under the correct response. This gives them early training in standardized test-taking.

#3-14

Personal Stories: A Book for Adults Who Are Beginning to Read, Books 1, 2 and 3 (1985) by Kamla Devi Koch, Linda Mrowicki and Arlene Ruttenberg. Palatine: Linmore Publishing. Book 1 is 78pp, ISBN 0-916591-02-6. Audio cassette tapes and a teacher's book are available for each level.

These are very systematic readers with exercises for literacy students. After a student has worked on the story with a teacher or tutor, he or she can write the exercises independently. The stories are high interest, with ongoing episodes about the same people. The books are inexpensive.

#3-15

Practice with Your Partner: A Kit of Student-Student Interaction Activities (1987) by Linda Mrowicki. Palatine: Linmore Publishing. 46pp. ISBN 0-916591-09-3.

This is a set of student cards with an accompanying teacher's book. The cards include dates, times, phone numbers, etc., which students can dictate to partners. The cards are intended for practice, not initial instruction. They are organized in order of difficulty within a given topic, so that students can work at different levels. They allow students to engage in meaningful pairwork from the very beginning.

See also:
Real-Life English, item #2-5 in the *Coursebooks* section.

#3-16

Start Right: A Positive Approach to Literacy (1991) by Karen Brinkman and Joanie Walker. Paramus: Prentice Hall, now Pearson Education. 176pp. ISBN 0-13-068271-3. (If not ordering through your school, orders for this title must be placed through a bookstore.)

This book uses a combination of approaches, such as photographs, Total Physical Response and Language Experience to teach literacy. However, it provides less context and is less connected to the lives of adult ESL students than the books by Sharron Bassano item #3-11) and Linda Mrowicki (item #s 3-12, 3-13, 3-14, 3-15, 3-17).

#3-17

Starting to Read (1988) by Linda Mrowicki. Palatine, IL: Linmore. 84pp. ISBN 0-916591-11-5. A teacher's book and an audio cassette tape are also available.

This is a very systematic, highly structured literacy book. It is good for volunteer tutors working one-on-one with students as well as for a class. Students can do some of the exercises on their own after being introduced to a lesson. There is plenty of practice in reading and writing. At the end of each lesson students write about themselves. This book would be used after *First Words* (item #3-12 above). The student book contains a scope and sequence chart, which is useful in planning lessons. There is a very helpful, though brief, teacher's guide that includes ways to personalize the lessons and suggestions for using the book in a multilevel class.

#3-18

Take Charge! A Student-Centered Approach to English, **Books 1 and 2 (1997) by Edna T. Diolata. New York: McGraw-Hill. Book 1 is 140pp, ISBN 0-07-044427-7. A grammar workbook, teacher's manual and audio cassette tape are available for each level.**

This series seeks to blend beginning literacy instruction with zero level speaking and listening skills. What we like about the material is that the exercises are always personalized. The students are involved in pairwork and interaction from the very beginning and throughout the book. Even at this beginning level they ask each other real questions and share their personal experiences. They also do information-gap exercises together, as well as practice giving commands and performing actions.

There is a pleasing variety of activities here, most of them quite short yet involving all the language skills. The text is uncluttered and not overwhelming. Clear line drawings illustrate each page, not just to help teach new vocabulary, but also to help the students talk about actions and their own likes and dislikes. We like the picture stories, in which students listen to a story and number the pictures in the correct order. They retell the story, then write it down (some words are already given). Finally, they write about themselves based on the story's format.

The book provides a good starting point for a course and would be pleasant to teach from. Some students will need additional material for further practice on literacy skills.

#3-19

Very Easy True Stories: A Picture-Based First Reader **(1998) by Sandra Heyer. White Plains: Addison Wesley Longman, now Pearson Education. 90pp. ISBN 0-201-34313-4.**

These are 14 very interesting human-interest stories for students who are familiar with the alphabet but who have low-level literacy skills. The stories will catch anyone's interest: A couple is trapped in an elevator, fall in love and later marry; a man finds $2,000 in his lunch bag. Each story is presented first with a picture to introduce the vocabulary. Then, the story is told step-by-step in a dozen or so cartoon frames with captions. Finally, the story is told again in text format. Some literacy is necessary to read these stories, but students who are just learning to read will be thrilled to be reading something "real." Some comprehension and practice exercises are provided but the real usefulness of this text is in the stories themselves—teachers and students alike enjoy them. (This is the first in a series of five *True Stories* readers; see *Reading*, Chapter 6, for more.)

CHAPTER 4

Teaching Activities

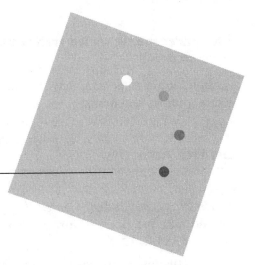

ESL teachers are always looking for activities that will spice up their lessons, vary the routine and provide a change of pace for their students. Experienced teachers keep a file of these "fill-in" or additional activities which they can pull out when needed. In this section we list the most useful collections of activities we know about. Most of these resource books are written by experienced teachers; consequently, the activities have been tried out in real classes and found to be successful.

The best ESL activities are not just fluff or time-wasters! They should be linked to the other work students are doing in class—perhaps practicing the same vocabulary or structures or expanding a textbook lesson. For example, if your class is studying the topic of family, you can find many activities, such as drawing family trees, role-playing, or puzzles, to expand that topic and make it more fun and interesting. In selecting an activity for your students, remember that it should provide some real communication practice to be most beneficial. Ideally, a good activity also requires the students to use several different language skills.

Pick and choose

Many of the books we have listed below are reproducible, that is, the purchaser has permission to photocopy activities from the book for classroom use. Usually they are not intended to be used sequentially like a textbook, but to be "dipped into" selectively. As you look at a particular resource book, you may not find activities directly related to your content or level but you may be able to find some ideas that can easily be adapted to your own students' needs. It is worth having some of these resources available in your library so that you can locate appropriate activities when you need them. You will find more activities like these listed under specific topics, such as our *Reading, Writing* and *Speaking and Listening* sections.

In addition to general activities books, this unit includes sections on visuals, games, puzzles and music.

General Activities

#4-1

Action Plans: 80 Student-Centered Language Activities (1984) by Marion MacDonald and Sue Rogers-Gordon. Rowley: Heinle & Heinle Publishers. 89pp. ISBN 0-8384-2712-X.

> This slim book has clear descriptions of many useful activities to expand the students' participation. For example, in 'Picture Narrative,' students in small groups select a picture and write a story about it. They read this to the rest of the class and then pose comprehension questions to the other students. Many of these activities are classics in the field. The book might be most interesting to teachers new to ESL.

#4-2

Back and Forth: Pair Activities for Language Development (1985, 1998) by Adrian S. Palmer, Theodore S. Rodgers with Judy Winn-Bell Olsen. San Francisco: Alta Book Center Publishers. 110pp. ISBN 1-882483-73-1.

> Most of the activities in this book are simple, information-gap style exercises in which students look at simple drawings and take turns describing and identifying these to each other. (There are about sixteen of these activities with two full reproducible pages each.) As they work, students correct each other, which is a benefit of this type of exercise. These would be fun to do and would be useful for pre-class warmup or for a short break between lessons.

See also:

Caring and Sharing (item #1-10 in the *Methods* section) for humanistic activities you can adapt to any classroom.

Cathy's Cards (item #5-9 in the *Speaking* section), which provides a fun way to get students talking.

#4-3

Communication Starters and Other Activities for the ESL Classroom (1977, 1990) by Judy Winn-Bell Olsen. Prentice Hall Regents, now Pearson Education. 129pp. ISBN 0-13-155656-8.

> Although this book, written over 20 years ago, is practically an antique in our field (the original edition even looks like it was produced on a typewriter!), it is still a valuable source of ideas for practical classroom activities. For ex-

ample, the book has a nine-page section on ways to use Cuisenaire rods (small blocks of different colors and sizes usually used to teach math) in language teaching. There is also a detailed section on teaching with maps, which you won't find anywhere else. There are also many ideas for game activities and activities using pictures. There are some reproducible activities, including a picture sequence about weddings. This book is useful for tutors as well as teachers, especially those new to the field.

#4-4

Drawing Out: Creative, Personalized, Whole Language Activities for Grades Five Through Adult (1982, 1995) by Sharron Bassano and Mary Ann Christison. San Francisco: Alta Book Center Publishers. 130pp. ISBN 1-882483-32-4.

This reproducible book has 54 one-page activities that all start with the student drawing something in the space provided. For example, "Draw a picture of a house in which you used to live." Following this are some questions that help the students get started on a short writing, i.e., "What did you like best about that house?" The students then share their drawings and discuss them. Another page with a follow-up activity, like an interview, gives students an opportunity to write or discuss more on the topic. A final chapter gives 17 ideas for classroom activities that don't require drawing—students cut out pictures from magazines to complete these.

These activities could provide you with a lot of low-key starters for writing activities or for conversation. The student-created materials that result can be recycled and used again as lesson material. This book is most useful for lower level students but the idea of drawing before speaking or writing works with any level of student.

#4-5

Five-Minute Activities: A Resource Book of Short Activities (1992) by Penny Ur and Andrew Wright. Cambridge: Cambridge University Press. 105pp. ISBN 0-521-39781-2.

This is a handy book with a variety of short activities for those days when your planned lesson is not quite long enough or you are asked at the last minute to teach a class. Many of the activities provide a useful way to review vocabulary or to introduce a new topic. There are several simple interaction activities that provide students with an opportunity to get to know each other better. For example, in one activity pairs of students try to find out how many things they have in common, and report the results starting with "We both. . . ." These activities are suitable for high beginners and up (levels are not indicated in the instructions). Most require a minimum of preparation and materials. This is an especially useful resource for new teachers who don't yet have their own "repertoire" of such activities.

#4-6

Games for Language Learning, Second Edition (1979, 1984) by Andrew Wright, David Betteridge and Michael Buckby. Cambridge: Cambridge University Press. 224pp. 0-521-27737-X.

This very useful book includes many kinds of language learning games, such as picture games, guessing games, sound games, story games. Many of these are really techniques that you can use over and over in different lessons. For example, 'Kim's Game' is a fun vocabulary activity, useful for reviewing the names of any objects. The activities are easily adapted to a particular teaching situation or level. This is a resource to turn to when you really need something fun to spice up a lesson.

See also:

Grammar Games and *Grammar Practice Activities* (items #8-4 and #8-5 in the *Grammar* chapter).

#4-7

Hands-on English, a periodical for teachers and tutors of adult ESL, Anna Silliman, editor. Crete, NE: Hands-on English. Six issues a year, 16 pages each. ISSN 1056-2680.

This publication comes out six times a year with practical, ready-to-use activities for adult ESL. Many activities have a photocopiable worksheet; some are suggestions for your "idea file." Most of the activities are designed for beginning through intermediate students, and some literacy level activities are included. Regular features are a multilevel crossword puzzle and multilevel dictations. Articles and ideas are contributed by teachers.

#4-8

Index Card Games for ESL, Second Edition (1982, 1992) by Raymond C. Clark and Ruthanne Brown. Brattleboro: Pro Lingua Associates. 80pp. ISBN 0-86647-052-2.

This little book describes six low-stress language learning games that belong in the repertoire of every ESL teacher and tutor. They are useful for any level of student, but especially for beginners and literacy level students. For example, scrambled sentences are useful for reviewing word order and focusing on meaning. Lots of word lists, sentences and paragraphs are given as example games but you can also use these techniques with any vocabulary your students are working on. There are clear instructions and many ideas for variations. If you haven't tried these before, you will want to run out and buy some blank 3x5 index cards right away.

#4-9

Interactive Techniques for the ESL Classroom (1991) by Connie L. Shoemaker and F. Floyd Shoemaker, New York: Newbury House/Heinle & Heinle Publishers. 162pp. IBN 0-8384-2671-9.

The introduction to this book contains succinct, easy to read background information on adult ESL teaching. This very helpful chapter explains clearly some of the special characteristics of adult learners.

The remainder of the book consists of communicative activities, divided into sections according to the type of activity (puzzles, games, roleplays, simulations, etc.). The activities are generally interesting, with a bit more depth than those in some other books. For example, one game has student groups bargaining with each other for resources to complete a task. A conversation activity has students practicing changing the subject (and other conversation skills) while they discuss a topic of interest. These activities are probably most useful for intermediate or advanced students, although many could be adapted for beginners. The authors identify affective and linguistic purposes for each activity; the extensive index and appendixes identify activities by level, content, and grammar point, among others.

#4-10

The Interactive Tutorial: An Activity Parade: Photocopyable Activities for the Adult ESL/EFL Student (1998) by Karen M. Sanders. Brattleboro: Pro Lingua Associates. 90pp. ISBN 0-86647-107-3.

This is a very accessible book for tutors working with adult ESL/EFL students at the beginning to low intermediate level. It includes simple interviews, information-gap exercises to do in pairs, card games, board games, and other activities designed to get students talking. The activities are easy to do. Not all the drawings are clear so you may need to discuss these carefully with the student.

In the table of contents, each activity is listed along with the theme it teaches and its level. They are grouped according to what the participants are asked to do: guessing, giving opinions, etc. The introduction includes suggestions for tutors about working with students (e.g., what to do about correction). The activities engage the tutor and the student in interaction and provide models for the tutor to make additional activities. There are blank game forms at the end of the book, which you can use to design your own games. The activities can also be used in a class setting.

#4-11

Live Action English, Third Edition (1979, 1997) by Elizabeth Romijn and Contee Seely. Berkeley: Command Performance Language Institute; available from book distributors. 96pp. ISBN 0-929724-16-X.

This is a collection of 67 action sequences, ranging from 12 to 18 sentences in length, describing common processes like writing a letter or going to the movies in a step-by-step manner. These sequences can be used in any number of ways in the classroom, especially for TPR (Total Physical Response) lessons in which students actually do the steps in class. Small illustrations of some vocabulary items are included. The introductory material is short but helpful, and includes a section on working with very low level students.

Many of the sequences correlate exactly to the picture sequences in *Action English Pictures* (item #4-21) and the two texts can be used to supplement each other.

#4-12

Operations in English, 55 Natural and Logical Sequences for Language Acquisition (1993) by Gayle Nelson and Thomas Winters. Brattleboro: Pro Lingua Associates. 104pp. ISBN 0-86647-074-3.

These are sequences, usually 8 to 10 sentences each, that describe an action, such as using a calculator, potting a plant, making spaghetti and using a fax machine. The sequences can be used for TPR (Total Physical Response) style lessons in which the students learn the vocabulary by performing the actions. They can also be used for many listening, speaking, reading and writing activities. Teaching suggestions and variations are provided in the book.

The benefit of this type of lesson for beginning students is that it focuses more attention on learning new verbs than most language lessons, which tend to emphasize objects. Objects are easier to teach because you can point to them; an 'operation' sequence gives you a way to demonstrate verbs in context.

#4-13

Purple Cows and Potato Chips: Multi-Sensory Language Acquisition Activities (1987; 1995) by Mary Ann Christison and Sharron Bassano. San Francisco: Alta Book Center Publishers. 104pp. ISBN 1-882483-31-6.

This book of short, low-stress activities focuses on the senses: seeing, touching, hearing, smelling and tasting. The activities are engaging and will stimulate conversation in class. Most are not appropriate for true beginners because of the complexity of instructions and the linguistic requirements of the activities, but will work with high beginners and up.

Some examples of the activities: students follow instructions to fold an origami pattern; students listen to sounds and identify them; students categorize and identify smells; students look at a picture then try to remember the details. Many of these have a reproducible worksheet. We like the 'Preference Grids' in which students arrange a list of things according to their likes and dislikes. These activities might be a good choice when your classes need a calming interlude.

#4-14

The Recipe Book (1990) Seth Lindstromberg, editor. Harlow: Longman/Pilgrims, now Pearson Education. 92pp. ISBN 0-582-03764-6.

This is a very useful book of communicative activities, including warmups, role-plays and story-telling activities developed by many experienced teachers. Some of these emphasize language practice, for example one in which students describe their imaginary country. Others are intended to get students laughing and relaxed, such as one in which students point to an object and say the wrong word for it. There are activities at various levels that can be adapted for different themes. They require little preparation and copying. Some of the activities may appear a bit risky to newcomers to communicative activities but they are worth trying. (See also *The Standby Book*, #4-16.)

#4-15
Shenanigames, Grammar-Focused Interactive ESL/EFL Activities and Games (1997) by James Kealey and Donna Inness. Brattleboro: Pro Lingua Associates. 152pp. ISBN 0-86647-100-6.

This book gives you activities to help intermediate students practice certain grammar structures. Many of these are information-gap type activities. For example, to practice *too* and *enough*, the students piece together information they have about someone named Ron, to find out how old he is and how much money he has in his pocket (Hint: He is old enough to vote). To practice prepositional phrases of location, students have a blank map of a town and have to find out from each other where the main buildings are (Hint: The restaurant is next to the courthouse). We think students will like these kinds of problem-solving activities.

#4-16
The Standby Book: Activities for the Language Classroom (1997) by Seth Lindstromberg, editor. Cambridge: Cambridge University Press. 249pp. ISBN 0-521-55860-3.

Like *The Recipe Book* (#4-14 above), this is a collection of communicative activities written by a number of authors. Many of these activities are more extensive in terms of classroom time needed, and they are best for intermediate or advanced students, although some can be adapted for beginners. The book includes sections of activities relating to specific kinds of classroom materials (coursebooks, readers) and one for teaching business people.

#4-17
Tasks for Independent Language Learning (1996) by David Gardner and Lindsay Miller, eds. Alexandria: Teachers of English to Speakers of Other Languages, Inc. 300pp. ISBN 0-939791-65-X.

This is a great resource for those who are tutoring, organizing independent learning centers or are seeking ways to teach multilevel classes. It describes activities for students working alone or in small groups in an easy to follow format.

See also:
Teaching Adult Second Language Learners (item #1-5 in the *Methods* section) for lots of activities on real life topics.

#4-18

Word Ways Cubes: For Oral Language Development (1979) by Bryan Benson and Lydia Stack. San Francisco: Alta Book Center Publishers. 22pp, plus 10 pre-printed cards. ISBN 0-88084-031-5.

We have used this simple, game-like activity for pre-class warm ups. Although it may look like 'kid stuff', it works great with adults. You assemble a simple cardboard cube—the one we like best has *who, what, why, where* and *when* on the sides. Students sit together in small groups and take turns rolling the cube and forming a question with the word that comes up. Another student answers the question, then takes a turn. We found this to be a low-key, structured way for students to get to know each other better.

Many suggestions are given with other cubes for practicing different grammar constructions; even weather and time. *Gameboards* and *Game Cards* are available from the same authors.

Visuals

#4-19

1,000 Pictures for Teachers to Copy (1984, 1985) by Andrew Wright. Reading: Addison-Wesley/Collins ELT, now Pearson Education. 128pp. ISBN 0-201-09132-1.

This is a great book for teachers who believe they can't draw but need to make rough sketches in class to convey meaning. The author shows how to make clear stick figures and caricature drawings, and gives some basic ideas on how those drawings can be used in the classroom. There are many pages that illustrate 20 or so adjectives, verbs, etc. You could copy these and use them as a reference/learning tool for your students, or you could produce similar pages yourself. Some of the 'Settings' (Bank, Post Office, Park) are useful, too.

#4-20

A Picture is Worth . . . 1000 Words, Books 1 and 2 (1992) by Anthony Mollica. Welland, Ontario: Editions Soleil Publishing Company; available from Delta Systems. Book 1 has 60 photos in both large and small formats, ISBN 0-921831-08-0. A teacher's guide is available for each book.

This book has a wonderful collection of provocative black and white photographs which may be reproduced. Each one has human-interest content and can be the basis of a description or story, either for conversation or writing. The photos can also be used to practice questions and modals since each picture has an element of uncertainty. For example: Why is the woman crying in Photo 35? Who is the man with her? Why does he look worried? What happened? Where are they going? Book 2 provides additional pictures. The teacher's guide has good suggestions for using the pictures, as well as specific discussion questions for each photo. This material is useful for almost any level.

#4-21

Action English Pictures: Activities for Total Physical Response (1985) by Noriko Takahashi and Maxine Frauman-Prickel. San Francisco: Alta Book Center Publishers. 110pp. ISBN 1-882483-71-5.

This book is based on the Total Physical Response (TPR) approach to language teaching, in which students act out the material they are learning. The book provides over 80 sequences of action in pictures. For example, a sequence on changing a light bulb has 12 pictures in which we see a man attempt to turn on a light, realize the bulb is burned out, find a new bulb, unplug the lamp, screw in the new bulb, etc. The book has a good introduction to TPR and how to use the picture sequences. It also provides model lessons. This is a good way to get beginners actively involved in their class.

AS: "When I was tutoring a beginning student with low literacy skills we used some of these sequences. There was a lot of new vocabulary for her but she really liked them. She could take the pictures and practice talking about them at home."

#4-22

The Card Book: Interactive Games and Activities for Language Learners (1991) by Abigail Tom and Heather McKay. San Francisco: Alta Book Center Publishers. 146pp. ISBN 1-882483-79-0.

This book includes nine sets of 27 simple picture cards each (a total of 243 picture cards) which can be photocopied. They are arranged by themes, such as clothing, food, road signs and furniture. Students can cut the pictures out, label them and use them to practice vocabulary in class and out. Once the basic vocabulary is learned, though, the real fun is in the interactive activities that accompany the picture sets. For example, in one activity students bargain with each other to "buy" and "sell" their clothing cards at the best price.

Even beginning and literacy level students can participate in the problem solving, information sharing and opinion sharing activities provided here.

See also:

Chalk Talks (item #5-1 in the *Speaking* section), which gives teachers a technique for transmitting student stories with simple pictures.

#4-23

Comics and Conversation: Using Humor to Elicit Conversation & Develop Vocabulary (1985) by Joan Ashkenas. Studio City, CA: JAG Publications. ISBN 0-943327-00-8.

These wordless cartoon strip stories are suitable for high beginners and up. The stories are funny and interesting; their visual humor 'translates' well. Because the cartoons are wordless, students can tell or write the stories at their own levels. By looking at one frame at a time, students can practice prediction. One cartoon, for example, shows a man lying in the street between parked cars as a crowd gathers. Then a woman arrives in a car and he gets up and gives her the place he has been saving. *More Comics and Conversation* (1991) provides additional cartoon strips.

#4-24

Easy Visuals for English Language Teachers (1993, 1995) by Richard Romo and Boone Brinson. Lincolnwood: NTC/Contemporary. 152pp. ISBN 0-8442-0797-7.

There are a few rudimentary pictures to reproduce here, and some ideas for drawing to explain concepts. But the real purpose of this book is to show you how to integrate posters, flip cards, drawings, magazine pictures and charts into your lessons. For example, one chart to show the meaning of 24 different prepositions is given, with some suggested activities for using it. Two ways to show the relationship of frequency words are given, with several practice activities. We also like the idea of having students make poster collages from cut-out magazine pictures.

The book has a real 'kiddie' look, but give it a chance—there are some useful teaching ideas here that will work with all students.

#4-25

Look Again Pictures for Language Development and Lifeskills (1984; 1998) by Judy Winn-Bell Olsen. San Francisco: Alta Book Center Publishers. 112pp. ISBN 1-882483-70-7.

This book consists of 22 'find the difference' pictures on topics such as shopping, banking, transportation and housing. For example, Picture 8 shows four people waiting at a supermarket checkout counter, the clerk, a bagger and a lot of groceries. The bottom picture is almost the same but there are eight differences for the students to find and discuss. Follow-up exercises include filling out a form for a check-cashing card, categorizing meat and poultry products and some other vocabulary practice activities.

Although the drawings are not very sophisticated, they are clear enough for the students to understand easily. Each picture is accompanied by oral and written exercises, many of them with lifeskills content. The book is suitable for high beginning and intermediate students. AS: "Students always enjoy these and sometimes get competitive about finding the differences."

#4-26

Picture It! Sequences for Conversation (1978, 1981) John Dumicich, editor. Prentice Hall Regents, now Pearson Education. 208pp. ISBN 0-13-676149-6.

Many picture stories for ESL have a cartoony, child-like aspect, but the line art in these picture sequences is unique for its sophisticated, adult quality. The book is divided into 15 topics about daily life—changing a flat tire, shopping for a jacket, etc. Each story is told in 32 pictures with no words. Some text is supplied at the end of each chapter, and the teaching suggestions provide ideas for all-skills practice, but you could do almost any language activity at any level with these pictures.

See also:
Short Cuts (item #2-6 in the *Coursebooks* chapter) which uses colorful pictures for listening activities.

#4-27
Visuals for the Language Classroom (1991) by Andrew Wright and Sofia Haleem. London: Longman, now Pearson Education. ISBN 0-582-04781-1.

This practical book goes beyond the usual pictures and includes charts, maps and other kinds of visual representations teachers can make for their classes without spending a fortune. The authors give many teaching examples.

Further visual resources:

See also:
The *Multi-Media Resources* section (Chapter 12), as many of these items offer visual input for ESL lessons.

The *Picture Dictionaries* section (in Chapter 9), as many of these also have posters, charts, and transparencies available.

Games

The following are games that are often used or adapted by ESL instructors.

#4-28
Bingo.

Many teachers devise their own versions of Bingo, using numbers for very beginning students, or pictures and words for higher levels. The game can be useful for practicing discrete listening skills. There are some ideas for making your own Bingo games in *Games for Language Learning* (item #4-6 above).

#4-29
Charades.

No purchase necessary; students silently act out words or phrases for other students to guess. Great for vocabulary review.

#4-30
GRIDIT! A Grid Game Book for Communication (1998) by Eileen A. Schwartz. San Diego: MADA Studios. Available direct from MADA Studios, P.O. Box 927645, San Diego, CA 92192. Internet: www.gridit.com

The author has a great idea for a simple board game your students can use to practice and review any vocabulary and discuss many issues. For example, there is a grid on job success which includes qualities like "helpful," "cooperative," "responsible" and "honest" for the students to discuss. The book offers 30 categories of games on many topics. These are reproducible and ready to use. Blank grids are included so you can devise your own. The game is adaptable to any level; best suited to beginning and intermediate students.

#4-31
Just-A-Minute! The Game That Has Everyone Talking! (1982) by Elizabeth Claire. Saddle Brook NJ: Eardley Publications; available from book distributors. Ninety-six topic cards included. ISBN 0-13-513136-7.

This is a type of 'Password' game written especially for ESL students. Students get a card with a topic, such as *Body Parts* or *Things That Go Fast*, and a list of words about that topic. They try to describe one of the words to a partner who has to guess the word. For example, "You listen with these." This game gives students good practice in explaining something, and it works well with high beginners through high intermediate students. Great for a 10 or 15 minute activity once in a while.

#4-32
Pictionary™ (available where games are sold).

This commercially available party game was popular a few years ago and many ESL teachers brought it into their classrooms for special events. Students play in teams; one student takes a card with a word on it and tries to get the other students to guess the word by sketching a picture on the blackboard. This can get pretty silly, and so would be fun for an end-of-the-year party, for example.

#4-33
Scrabble™ (available where games are sold).

This well-known, commercially available game is often adapted by ESL teachers. Advanced students can play with regular rules. Intermediate students can play by choosing a larger number of pieces to make words from, and beginning students can work together to make as many interconnected words as they can with all the available pieces. Students can then copy the results onto a sheet of paper and make a crossword puzzle with it.

#4-34
Talk about Trivia, 1001 Questions (1986) by Irene Schoenberg. White Plains: Longman, now Pearson Education. 117pp. ISBN 0-582-90721-7.

This book is written especially for ESL students. You can use it for conversation about interesting aspects of American culture, or for a 'Trivial Pursuit' type board game which the students can play together. There are six categories of questions: *General Knowledge about the U.S., Phrases and Idioms, American Holidays, Vocabulary, American History* and *Grammar.* The questions are interesting and amusing. For example, "The city best known for gambling is: a) Las Vegas b) Los Angeles c) Miami Beach." Part One of the book is for high beginning or low intermediate students, and Part Two is for intermediate or high intermediate students. AS: "My students really enjoyed this material! They didn't want to stop playing when class was over."

Puzzles

#4-35
Solo, Duo, Trio, Puzzles and Games for Building English Language Skills (1997) by Richard Yorkey. Brattleboro: Pro Lingua Associates. 166pp. ISBN 0-86647-091-3.

The author designed these puzzles for students to work on their own—this is useful if you have a multilevel class and some students need an extra activity. The puzzles include word search puzzles, 'jumbled stories,' crossword puzzles, acrostics, riddle puzzles and more. The level is appropriate for low intermediate through high intermediate. Many of the puzzles are short and would not take much time to complete; all are reproducible.

#4-36
Thematic Activities for Beginners in English (1995) by John F. Chabot. Virgil, Ontario: Full Blast Productions. ISBN 1-895451-16-7.

Most of the activities in this book are 'pencil puzzles' which beginning students can do on their own. There are crosswords, wordsearch puzzles, scrambled words and words with missing letters, all on a related theme such as clothing, animals, transportation, etc. Word lists are illustrated with small drawings, so students can review the vocabulary. Although these activities are not communicative, students always seem to enjoy focusing on word puzzles as a break from more open-ended work.

Further puzzle resources:

You can make your own wordsearch puzzles based on vocabulary your students are learning in class using an inexpensive computer program such as *Wordsearch Studio*, available from Educational Resources (item #13-8 in the *Publisher* section).

For do-it-yourself crossword puzzles, one computer program is called *Crossword Magic* by Mindscape Educational Software (available from Gessler Publishing Co., 1-800-456-5825, *www.gessler.com*). Several other crossword puzzle programs for teachers are available (see Educational Resources, #13-8).

See also:
Hands-on English (item #4-7 above), which has multilevel puzzles in each issue.

Music

Teaching with songs seems to have gone out of fashion since our early teaching days, and many good old songbooks are no longer in print. Perhaps the trend will soon swing back the other way, and we can offer you more music resources in our next edition of this book!

#4-37

Sing it! Learn English Through Song Books 1–6 (1994) by Millie Grenough. McGraw-Hill. Book 1 text is ISBN 007-024705-6. Books 1 through 6 available with an audio cassette tape for each.

This series provides musical selections of interest to adults, with a reading passage about the origin of each one, a score to sing from, and several vocabulary, grammar and comprehension exercises. The music is from a wide range of genres including traditional folk (*Clementine*), modern folk (*We Shall Overcome*), spiritual (*Go Tell It on the Mountain*), songs from stage (*Summertime*) and screenplays (*Oh What a Beautiful Morning*), early rock (*I Want to Hold Your Hand*), and popular songs (*Georgia on My Mind*) as well as love songs and other contemporary numbers. Over 80 pieces are included in all.

The songs are presented with sensitivity and warmth. The cultural information is interesting, as well as the highlights of artists and singers. The cassette recordings are clear and make it easy to sing along. The series is suitable for high beginners and up, and is sequenced according to level of difficulty and verb tense. This series would make a nice supplement to regular class work and is also a great resource for substitute teacher lessons.

CHAPTER 5

Speaking and Listening

Many teachers and students see speaking and listening as the heart of their classes. In lower level classes, students usually listen to and say the same materials they read and write. Their speaking activities are much more structured. Coursebooks, in general, often integrate speaking with the other skills and provide audio tapes for listening practice. At higher levels or in conversation courses, separate listening and speaking materials, such as those in this chapter, are useful in helping students focus on specific skills.

We have divided this chapter into three sub-sections, *Speaking/Conversation*, *Listening* and *Pronunciation*, each with a separate introduction.

Speaking/Conversation

Coursebooks usually include speaking activities as part of an integrated language learning plan. But most teachers are still always looking for good ways to get their students talking, and for more ways to develop students' speaking skills. In this section we've included materials that might provide this kind of supplement.

Many of the following conversation books give the teacher ideas and materials to use in a conversation class or for the conversation component of more general classes, from beginning level through intermediate. These materials can also be useful for tutors working with individuals or small groups at these levels. Higher level students are often able to take more responsibility for a conversation class by introducing their own topics and materials.

Speaking/Conversation: Teacher Resources

#5-1

Chalk Talks (1994) by Norma Shapiro and Carol Genser. Berkeley: Command Performance Language Institute; available from book distributors (see Chapter 13). 190pp. ISBN 0-929724-15-1.

How do you get zero level or beginning students communicating in English? The authors have an ingenious technique of drawing symbols or stick figures on the chalkboard to express what the student is saying. These are then turned into a language lesson. This lesson can help the student tell his or her story, which the other students can discuss and practice too. For example, a student came to class with a sprained ankle. The teacher elicited, with questions, the story of how it happened, and drew six pictures that explained the story. Using these pictures, the students could learn new vocabulary, retell the story, ask questions and discuss related issues.

Thirty-two prepared lessons are included in the book, which you can use either just as they are or as inspiration for your own lessons. The introduction gives many wonderful tips on eliciting stories and drawing symbols so that you can incorporate this technique into your own teaching. The ultimate in student-centered learning, this book should receive some kind of award.

#5-2

Conversation (1987) by Rob Nolasco and Lois Arthur. Oxford: Oxford University Press. 148pp. ISBN 0-19-437096-8.

This book offers many practical suggestions about teaching conversation as well as numerous activities. There are few activities for true beginners; most are suitable for intermediate and higher levels. There is a nice section on helping students reflect on the language they hear and use. This is a good resource for an intermediate or advanced conversation class.

#5-3

Conversation Inspirations: Over Two Thousand Conversation Topics, Second Edition, Revised (1986, 1996) by Nancy Ellen Zelman. Brattleboro: Pro Lingua Associates. 128pp. ISBN 0-86647-094-8.

This classic resource, originally published in 1986, provides an endless supply of ideas for conversations, role-plays, interviews, etc. This is useful for any conversation class or discussion group at an intermediate level or higher, and is a 'must-have' for any teacher who does substitute teaching and is looking for ideas.

#5-4

Discussions that Work: Task Centered Fluency Practice (1981) by Penny Ur. Cambridge: Cambridge University Press. 122pp. ISBN 0-521-28169-5.

This classic work has a very useful introductory section which provides general principles for planning class discussions, including identifying a topic, grouping students and setting and organizing the task. There is a brief but very useful section on roleplay. The author also includes many examples of brainstorming activities (for example students are given an object and asked to list as many uses for it as possible), and good ideas for organizing-type activities (for example students have to decide how to re-arrange a zoo to solve certain problems with the animals). This book is most useful for teachers of intermediate and advanced classes and conversation classes.

#5-5
Focus on Speaking (1997) by Anne Burns and Helen Joyce. Sydney: National Center for English Language Teaching and Research; available from book distributors. 137pp. ISBN 1-86408-297-6.

The first part of this Australian book is theoretical, but each bit of theory is followed by a section called *Implications for Teaching*, which helps the reader apply what he or she has read. There is a good section on organizing a speaking course or a speaking component of a more general course and one on assessing speech.

#5-6
Keep Talking: Communicative Fluency Activities for Language Teaching (1984) by Friederike Klippel. Cambridge: Cambridge University Press. 202pp. ISBN 0-521-27871-6.

This is a classic book of activities for pair and small group work. There are a lot of good teaching ideas here, organized into three main types of activity: questions and answers, discussions and decisions and stories and scenes. The index lists activities by function and grammar but not by content.

Speaking/Conversation: Student Materials

#5-7
All Clear! Intro: Speaking, Listening, Expressions, and Pronunciation in Context (1998) by Helen Kalkstein Fragiadakis. Boston: Heinle & Heinle Publishers. 200pp. ISBN 0-8384-6030-5.

This text for high beginners seeks to teach them common expressions we use in everyday life, for example "I can't wait," "I'll be right back," "That sounds great," etc., which are useful in the most basic situations. Each lesson presents 8 to 10 new expressions in a conversation; for example two people discussing plans for the weekend. Some listening exercises help the students understand the dialogue, then each of the expressions ("Go away" for example) is explained in detail, with several more examples given in dialogue form. For each entry, there is a short interactive exercise in which students practice the expression in pairs (i.e., "Do you like to go away?"). Some pronunciation and listening exercises follow, then a short writing exercise to review the expressions. An open-ended conversation activity gives students a chance to try using these themselves.

We think this book does a good job of presenting useful expressions in contexts that are realistic and relevant enough that students will learn them and use them. Check-off sheets at the end of each chapter help students quantify how much they are learning, which is very satisfying for students at this level.

#5-8

All Sides of the Issue: Activities for Cooperative Jigsaw Groups (1989, 1998) by Elizabeth Coelho, Lise Winer and Judy Winn-Bell Olsen. San Francisco: Alta Book Center Publishers. 154pp. ISBN 1-882483-72-3.

This book has a good introduction to cooperative learning and the jigsaw approach, in which students work in groups on a particular piece of material. They then take their information to new groups, where members share what they have learned in their separate groups and work together to solve a problem. For example, in *Saving the Biramichi River,* a chemical company and a commercial fishery try to work out a way to co-exist on the same river. The reading materials are suitable for a low intermediate or higher class. In each activity, two of the readings are easier than the other two, making this useable for a mixed level class. AS: "Because the activities are in-depth they are more time consuming than many other typical ESL activities. They would be difficult to use in a class with short teaching periods and where attendance is erratic."

#5-9

Cathy's Cards: Instant Conversation in the Classroom, Adult Edition (1996) by Cathy Seitchik Diaz. San Francisco: Alta Book Center Publishers. 270 question cards. ISBN 1-882483-36-7.

This is a simple but useful conversation tool for teachers at all levels. Each of the cards has an opinion or human-interest type question, ranging from "What kind of shampoo do you use?" to "What are three of the most important things in your life?" This material provides a good way to get students talking and interacting even if they don't know each other very well. Just hand out the cards and let the students talk.

#5-10

A Conversation Book 1: English in Everyday Life, Third Edition, Revised (1977, 1998) by Tina Kasloff Carver and Sandra Douglas Fotinos. Englewood: Prentice Hall Regents, now Pearson Education. Book 1 is 258pp, ISBN 0-13-792433-X. A teacher's guide, audio cassette tapes, testing materials and transparencies are also available. Book 2 provides the same set of materials.

This colorful book illustrated with lively drawings provides everyday vocabulary and activities for practicing it. It is organized around topics such as food, housing and health. The teacher's guide is very thorough and provides the novice teacher with a great many communicative activities that are not in the student book. It is worth looking at for all levels. AS: "I think some of the small picture sequences are hard to understand."

See also:
Conversations in English (item #2-2 in the *Coursebooks* section) for speaking activities.

#5-11
Culturally Speaking: A Conversation and Culture Text, **Second Edition (1986, 1994) by Rhona B. Genzel and Martha Graves Cummings. Boston: Heinle & Heinle Publishers. 193pp. ISBN 0-8384-4213-7. An audio cassette tape is also available.**

This is a high intermediate or advanced reading and discussion book through which students explore aspects of North American life and culture while they practice speaking. In each chapter, several model dialogues (in the text and also on the tape) present the material to students, for example making a purchase at a department store or making a mail-order purchase by telephone. Each chapter also includes many communicative activities such as roleplaying (for example, returning an item to a store). Students are encouraged to seek information in the community around them. The book would be useful for students who are beyond the simple survival stage but who need more details about how things work in American culture and appropriate ways to say things.

#5-12
Discussions A to Z: A Resource Book of Speaking Activities **Intermediate (1997) by Adrian Wallwork. Cambridge: Cambridge University Press. 112pp. ISBN 0-521-55981-2. An audio cassette tape is also available.**

This is a book of interesting bits and pieces to read, listen to and discuss, organized under topics such as jobs, time, and xenophobia. The intermediate level (an advanced level is also available) is suitable for advanced conversation classes for adults. The book's readings and illustrations are reproducible. Provocative questions for discussion and writing topics are included. The tape includes a variety of British and American voices speaking at normal speed.

#5-13
Functions of American English: Communication Activities for the Classroom **(1983) by Leo Jones and C. Von Baeyer. Cambridge: Cambridge University Press. 150pp. ISBN 0-521-28528-3. A teacher's manual and an audio cassette tape are also available.**

This is an advanced book based on language functions (starting a conversation, giving advice, complaining). Each unit provides a sample dialogue which students can listen to on tape as they read along, and introduces alternative phrases (for example, different ways to request someone's help). Several exercises and communication activities give students an opportunity to practice these. There is a lot of material in this book, and it may provide more choices than the students want—if so, you can just select those you wish to practice.

At the end of each chapter is a suggested communication activity in which students role-play (in pairs or small groups) a situation to practice the language functions they've learned. These are well thought-out and useful but they are not simple and plenty of classroom time should be allowed for them. AS: "This material was quite challenging for my high-intermediate students, but they really liked it."

#5-14

Listen and Say It Right in English: When to Use Formal and Everyday English (1988, 1992) by Nina Weinstein. Lincolnwood: NTC/Contemporary. Student book is 96pp, ISBN 0-8442-0450-5. A teacher's manual and audio cassette tapes are also available.

This is a book for advanced students who want to learn more about appropriate register. Each conversation is presented in a formal and an informal way. It may provide more alternatives than most students want. The book and cassettes come in one package along with a teacher's guide.

See also:

May I Help You? (item #10-8 in the *Workplace* section), which has good roleplay activities for students to practice the language needed for dealing with the public.

#5-15

Picture Stories: Language and Literacy Activities for Beginners (1990) by Fred Ligon and Elizabeth Tannenbaum with Carol Richardson Rodgers, in association with The Experiment in International Living. White Plains: Longman, now Pearson Education. 121pp. ISBN 0-8013-0366-4.

The stories in this book are told in a series of cartoon picture strips suitable for beginners but useable at all levels. The stories are about everyday activities such as shopping and going to the doctor, many with a slight humorous twist. Many of these are about mishaps—for example, a man goes into a phone booth to make a call, and while he is talking a thief steals his briefcase. The stories are very useful for building vocabulary and fluency. Students can tell or write the stories in their own words, or dictate them to another writer. There are exercises to check comprehension. *More Picture Stories* (1992) by the same authors provides additional picture stories and exercises. AT: "It's hard to categorize these books. My students tell the stories and then use them as a basis for collaborative writing."

#5-16

Problem Solving: Critical Thinking and Communication Skills (1991) by Linda W. Little and Ingrid A. Greenberg. White Plains: Longman, now Pearson Education. 128pp. ISBN 0-8013-0603-5.

This is a problem-posing, problem solving book using real problems of immigrants: family problems, money problems, work problems. Each lesson is introduced by a picture, which gives students a chance to predict the content.

The reading in each lesson is suitable for high beginning and intermediate students. There are questions to check comprehension and to aid in discussion of the topic. AT: "My high beginning students really like talking about these stories."

#5-17
Speaking Naturally: Communication Skills in American English (1985) by Bruce Tillitt and Mary Newton Bruder. Cambridge: Cambridge University Press. 115pp. ISBN 0-521-27130-4. An audio cassette tape is also available.

This conversation book is organized by functions (for example, invitations, apologizing, agreeing and disagreeing) and is very similar to *Functions of American English* (item #5-13 above) except that it is less complex and more suitable for intermediate and high-intermediate students. Students hear an extended dialogue, then they read a description about appropriate language, for example when to make compliments. They study some specific phrases, then practice them in small groups in structured, 'cued dialogues.' Finally, students practice the new language in open-ended roleplays. (For example, a co-worker is showing you pictures of the new baby. What do you say?) We think this material can be adapted nicely to suit your students. It is especially useful for students who want to learn about different levels of formality.

See also:
Speaking of Survival (item #10-3 in the *Survival Skills* section) for real-life conversation practice at the intermediate level on lifeskills topics.

#5-18
Talk About Values: Conversation Skills for Intermediate Students (1989) by Irene Schoenberg. White Plains: Longman, now Pearson Education. 105pp. ISBN 0-8013-0011-8.

This book explores cultural values about topics such as borrowing money, aging, smoking and sports. Within each topic students learn the kinds of things we do or don't say (i.e., Do I tell her I don't like the new dress?) and have a chance to talk about what they think is important (i.e., comfort or looks?). The exercises are short but they provide plenty of support (surveys, pair and small group discussions) for reluctant speakers. At the end of each topic, the authors provide suggestions for writing topics. The level is just right for intermediate students.

Further resources for Speaking/Conversation:

See also the *Activities* section (Chapter 4) for general classroom activities, many of which emphasize speaking skills.

Listening

Listening, as a skill, used to be taken for granted in language learning classes. Most emphasis was traditionally put on getting students to produce language (speaking and writing). More and more, though, educators are realizing that listening can and should be taught and practiced in the classroom. Like reading, listening can provide a lot of valuable language input to the student, as long as it is comprehensible. (It doesn't do any good to listen to something you can't understand.)

When selecting listening activities for your students, look for ones that have guides, charts or pictures to help focus the students' listening and make it easier for them to understand. Choose listening segments that are longer and have more of a context (such as a story) rather than those that are short and lack context. The context is what helps students understand the story and make sense of the new language in it.

Sources of input

Listening materials with tapes provide additional voices for students to listen to as well as strategies for listening. These are especially useful if they are 'authentic,' or natural-sounding. Such recorded speech can also provide a stimulus to class discussion. However, many sets of tapes are prohibitively expensive. Some teachers instead ask friends or family to help them record materials for class. Advanced students may prefer material taken directly from the radio or television.

Listening: Teacher Resources

#5-19
Dictation: New Methods, New Possibilities (1988) by Paul Davis and Mario Rinvolucri. Cambridge: Cambridge University Press. 122pp. ISBN 0-521-34819-6.

This book takes the old technique of dictation and provides a wealth of creative techniques for using it in the classroom. Some focus on individual words or sounds while others involve reconstructing text, making phone calls and telling stories. This is great for the adventurous teacher who wants to do something different.

#5-20
"Listening Comprehension in Second/Foreign Language Instruction," (1991) article by Joan Morley in *Teaching English as a Second or Foreign Language*, Marianne Celce Murcia, editor (see #1-8 in the *Methods* section).

This article includes an excellent description of the importance of listening in language teaching, some basic principles for teaching listening and some specific lessons.

#5-21

Listening in Action: Activities for Developing Listening in Language Teaching (1991) by Michael Rost. New York: Prentice Hall, now Pearson Education. 160pp. ISBN 0-13-538778-7.

This resource book provides good background information on listening. It includes useful activities which can be adapted to different students and situations. At the end of each activity there is a "teacher's diary section" with questions to help the teacher evaluate it.

#5-22

Teaching Listening Comprehension (1984) by Penny Ur. Cambridge: Cambridge University Press. 172pp. ISBN 0-521-28781-2.

This book begins with an excellent section on the kinds of listening people actually do, with suggestions about what to look for (and what to make up yourself) in classroom listening materials. It provides excellent activities for listening, some for perception (sounds, words) and others for comprehension, organized according to the kinds of responses required (none, short, long, discussion). It's a good introduction to listening for teachers at all levels.

Listening: Student Materials

#5-23

Basic Tactics for Listening (1996) by Jack C. Richards. New York: Oxford University Press. Student book is 72pp, ISBN 0-19-434587-4. A teacher's book and audio cassette tapes or audio CDs are also available.

This book is organized by topics (including family, small talk, restaurants and many others) and has several listening tasks within each topic, one for global listening and the others for more specific, directed listening. It provides good listening practice for intermediate level students. The topics may be more suitable for younger adults than for older students. Tapes or CDs and a teacher's book are available. *Developing Tactics for Listening* and *Expanding Tasks for Listening* are higher levels in the same series.

#5-24

Book One: Listening and Speaking Activities for Beginning Students of English (1997) by John R. Boyd and Mary Ann Boyd. Englewood Cliffs: Prentice Hall Regents, now Pearson Education. Student book is 112pp, ISBN 0-13-299785-1. A teacher's edition, and audio cassette tapes are also available.

This workbook of task-oriented listening exercises is useful for low-beginning students, and some of these would also be appropriate for literacy level students. For example, in an exercise to review colors, students look at a drawing of several racing cars. First the teacher asks a dozen questions like "What number is the orange car?" and the students write the number of that car on a worksheet. Next, the exercise is reversed and the teacher asks, "What color is car 19?" Students circle the correct color, then they write the word for that color. Another task has students circle the correct number when they hear a sentence like "332 million people speak Spanish," then they write these numbers as dictated. Because the exercises are very carefully graduated, they won't overwhelm beginners and may give them a sense of accomplishment. This book would be good to have on hand for an occasional paper-and-pencil activity to change the pace. (The teacher's book incorporates the tapescript.)

#5-25
Good News, Bad News: News Stories for Listening and Discussion (1997) by Roger Barnard. New York: Oxford University Press. Student book is 72pp, ISBN 0-19-434873-3. A teacher's book and audio cassette tapes or audio CDs are also available.

This intermediate level listening book is based on eighteen interesting true radio stories (similar to those in the *True Stories* series of reading books). One story is about a person who wins a lottery, another is about a prisoner escaping and a third is about a man who fell out of an ambulance. The accompanying tape or CD uses a variety of voices and accents and is reasonably priced. The exercises are well-written. Following the listening activities in each chapter is an oral activity for the class. There is also a teacher resource book with photocopiable activity and assessment pages as well as tapescripts.

#5-26
Improving Aural Comprehension (1972, 1976) by Joan Morley. Ann Arbor: University of Michigan Press. 297pp. ISBN 0-472-08665-0. A teacher's book and audio cassette tapes are also available.

This is a classic book on listening. The exercises are suitable for beginners and up and can be adapted or extended to include your own local information. It includes exercises on aural letter and number recognition as well as spatial and temporal relationships. Some of the tasks included are: discriminating between 40 and 14 (students circle the correct one), listening to a sentence and writing the numbers heard, listening to a number and finding it on a chart and taking dictation of addresses and phone numbers. Although these are not interactive activities, they are fun to work on and the tasks are satisfying to complete.

The teacher's manual is essential for the dictation scripts. A set of 11 cassettes is available but somewhat expensive. AT: "I just read the material to my class and often adapt it to my own situation (e.g., local addresses and phone numbers)."

#5-27
Intermediate Listening Comprehension: Understanding and Recalling Spoken English, Second Edition (1982, 1994) by Patricia Dunkel and Phyllis L. Lim. Boston: Heinle & Heinle Publishers. 176pp. ISBN 0-8384-4838-0.

Despite the title, we would use this text with an advanced class of adult students; that is, students who have fluent English and literacy skills but are not yet at an academic level. It is especially useful for students intending to go on to further study, as it teaches some useful rhetorical skills.

Each of the sixteen chapters is based on a "talk" about one subject such as why the dinosaurs disappeared, acid rain, the ancient city of Pompeii or hydroponic aquaculture. The students see a picture or diagram which helps them to follow the talk, and some vocabulary and pre-listening cues are given first to prepare them. The students listen again and take notes, then do comprehension exercises. Discussion questions give students a chance to express their opinions. Each chapter also has a follow-up listening activity using a map or chart. (An 'advanced' level by the same authors is also available.)

#5-28

Listen First: Focused Listening Tasks for Beginners (1991) by Jayme Adelson-Goldstein. New York: Oxford University Press. 88pp. ISBN 0-19-434422-3. A teacher's book and audio cassette tapes are also available.

This is a systematic and practical listening book for beginners with some literacy. It includes typical beginning level themes such as directions, health, clothing and employment. It also stresses different clarification strategies in each unit. A teacher's guide, containing transcripts of the recorded material, and a set of cassettes are available.

#5-29

Listening Tasks for Intermediate Students of English (1984) by Sandra R. Schecter. Cambridge: Cambridge University Press. 41pp. ISBN 0-521-27898-8. An audio cassette tape is available.

This is an excellent book of short, real-life listening tasks. Topics include banking, weather reports, directions and car repairs. Each listening task is accompanied by a short reading activity which extends the topic. The inexpensive cassette is essential for using the book. AT: "I really like this book. The lessons fit well with the themes I teach. I use some of them as a 'stretch' in my high beginning class."

#5-30

Listen to Me! Beginning Listening, Speaking, and Pronunciation. Second Edition (1985, 1994) by Barbara H. Foley. Boston: Heinle & Heinle Publishers. Student book is 115pp, ISBN 0-8384-5264-7. Audio cassette tapes are also available.

This book has 15 narratives, each one about the life of a different character. The students look at a drawing or series of drawings while they listen to the story. Then a series of exercises helps the students focus on meaning as they listen again. The stories mostly revolve around daily life and adult concerns, including job decisions, transportation issues, divorce, health concerns and a robbery. Several structure exercises, also based on listening, are included in each unit as well as one or two on pronunciation. A group discussion activity is also suggested. (This is the first in a series of three by the same author.)

#5-31

Moving On: Beginning Listening, Book 2 (1989) by Jann Huizenga and T. Forest. White Plains: Longman, now Pearson Education. 93pp. ISBN 0-8013-0119-X. An audio cassette tape is also available.

For very low beginners, this book has natural-sounding conversations about grocery shopping, the post office, a health clinic, etc. The students listen to the conversation while following the photographs that illustrate it. The vocabulary is all useful. Most of the comprehension exercises involve numbering photographs or checking them off. Follow-up activities give the students a chance to try the vocabulary themselves.

The first book in this series, *From the Start,* is for zero-level students and has nice exercises on money and counting but unfortunately we found some of the photographs too dark to see clearly. Book 3 in the series is called *Taking Off.*

#5-32

Now Hear This! High Beginning Listening, Speaking, and Pronunciation, Second Edition (1984, 1994) by Barbara H. Foley. Boston: Heinle & Heinle Publishers. 172pp. ISBN 0-8384-5270-1. Audio cassette tapes are also available.

This book has 15 interesting and realistic stories on current topics (for example, the Titanic, the World Trade Center bombing, winning the lottery, drunk driving, etc.) at the high beginning or low intermediate level. The students first see a photo or drawing and are given plenty of pre-listening exercises to prepare for the story. Then they listen to a segment that is a few minutes long. For example, Unit 1 is about two toll booth collectors, one of whom loves the job and the other hates it. The students talk about the story, then listen again for specific information. Several exercises follow, most of them intended to help the student focus on meaning (they don't need to comprehend every word). To follow up, some student interviews and group discussion activities are provided. While the exercises in this book are carefully structured and simple, the listening material is surprisingly natural and sophisticated for an ESL text. (This is second in a series of three by the same author. The third one, *Heart of the Matter,* not reviewed here, is a similar text for advanced students.)

#5-33

On the Air: Listening to Radio Talk (1998) by Catherine Sadow and Edgar Sather. New York: Cambridge University Press. 208pp. ISBN 0-521-65747-4. Audio cassette tapes are also available.

Although the book is described as being for intermediate level students, it would be more appropriate for advanced students in most adult programs. It has a nice mix of high-interest topics from radio programs. Each listening passage begins with background information on the speaker and is followed by discussion topics and exercises. A tape is available. AT: "The interviews are not too difficult for high intermediate students; the advertisements and call-in shows are appropriate for higher level students."

See also:
People at Work (item #10-9 in the *Workplace* section) which includes lengthy recorded interviews at an advanced level.

#5-34
Whaddaya Say? Guided Practice in Relaxed Spoken English (1983) by Nina Weinstein. Prentice Hall Regents, now Pearson Education. 80pp. ISBN 0-13-951708-1. A set of 2 audio cassette tapes is also available.

In most spoken English, reduced forms (gonna, wanna, hafta, gotta, etc.) are normal. Contrary to what students might think, these are not slang but are heard in every level of discourse. This book allows you to give students a careful introduction to reduced forms so that students will understand native speakers more easily. The dialogues in this book are entertaining, and the exercises are not difficult; probably low intermediate students can do them but higher levels may benefit, too.

The author does not intend that students should start producing these forms—the purpose of the material is to increase their listening comprehension. AS: "I've seen lots of students have an 'aha!' experience when they do these exercises."

Other sources for listening materials:

Telephone messages: Recorded phone messages make good listening practice and can help build student confidence. For example, time and temperature recordings, opening and closing times for public institutions, or days and dates for events are all available for the cost of a phone call.

Recorded books: Many companies offer books on audio cassette tapes and these are available for purchase in bookstores or can be borrowed from libraries. Most of these will be suitable only for advanced students; however one company we know of has material for schools that might possibly be useful for ESL students at lower levels: Recorded Books, Inc., 1-800-638-1304, www.recordedbooks.com/schools.asp.

See also:
Our section on *Reading for Pleasure* (in Chapter 6), which lists sources for many short readers with accompanying cassette tapes.

Pronunciation

We have never had much success in "teaching" pronunciation as a classroom topic. In our experience, pronunciation is best worked on as a continual thread throughout all of the other speaking and listening activities. When specific problems arise, though, it is helpful to have some information and resources available.

The pronunciation books included here range from those based on individual sounds or pairs of sounds to others focusing more on communication and longer speech samples. Some are suitable for students working on their own. The jazz chants are especially fun and relaxing, giving students a chance to practice English together.

Pronunciation: Teacher Resources

#5-35

Pronunciation Contrasts in English (1971, 1987) by Don L. F. Nilsen and Alleen Pace Nilsen. Prentice Hall Regents, now Pearson Education. 112pp. ISBN 0-13-730938-4.

This concise little reference book, originally published in 1971, is a helpful resource in pinpointing specific pronunciation problems for speakers of various languages. For example, under the listing for the *j/ch* contrast (as in *jest/chest*) you see a list of 25 languages for whose speakers this distinction might be difficult. Example sentences are given, and lists of English word pairs with the two sounds at the beginning, middle and end of the word. An index helps you locate problem sounds for each language.

We don't think that practicing 'minimal pairs' (that is, two words with contrasting sounds like *jest/chest*), necessarily helps students improve their pronunciation. It can, however, help them to identify sound distinctions in English that they weren't aware of.

#5-36

Pronunciation (1995) by Clement Laroy. Oxford: Oxford University Press. 135pp. ISBN 0-19-437087-9.

This is an unusual book about teaching pronunciation. Rather than pages full of face diagrams and contrasting pairs, it has holistic and multisensory pronunciation activities designed to help students take an active part in improving their pronunciation. It is divided into four sections. The first, *Tuning into Language*, helps students become more aware of what they hear. The second focuses on stress, rhythm and intonation. The third section encourages students to approach English sounds in a very personal way, by experimenting with sounds they can make and by "feeling the vowels," for example. The fourth section deals with correction, but again it's a very student-based approach, in which students try out sounds and correct themselves.

#5-37

Pronunciation Games (1995) by Mark Hancock. Cambridge: Cambridge University Press. 108pp. ISBN 0-521-46735-7.

This photocopiable book is unique among pronunciation resources in that it provides fun, interesting and visually-based activities for students to do while they are focusing on certain pronunciation issues. For example, 'Rhythm dominoes' helps students recognize stress patterns—they have to match phrases that have the same patterns. And a board game called 'Intonation monopoly' helps students practice intonation in question tags. We like the 'Contradict me' cards for students to practice contrastive stress. For example, "The formula for water is H-3-0." "You mean H-*TWO*-0." There are a few British points mentioned but the material is perfectly useful for North American English.

Most of the activities seem appropriate for intermediate through advanced level students. This is an innovative book you'll be glad you discovered.

Pronunciation: Student Materials

#5-38

Clear Speech: Pronunciation and Listening Comprehension in American English, Second Edition (1984, 1993) by Judy B. Gilbert. Cambridge: Cambridge University Press. Student's book is 144pp, ISBN 0-521-42118-7. A teacher's resource book and audio cassette tapes are also available.

The book is written for students with a high level of literacy and is best for students with some previous education. It could be used independently or in a class. Much of the emphasis is on learning to identify intonation and stress in individual words and sentences, with more focus on communication and context than is found in many pronunciation books. Cassettes are available as well as a teacher resource book. AS: "I found this book very helpful with intermediate or advanced level Asian students who had not been able to understand English intonation, stress and rhythms. It seemed to present these concepts very clearly for them."

#5-39

Get Ready: Interactive Listening and Speaking (1986) by Paul Abraham and Daphne Mackey. Englewood Cliffs: Prentice Hall Regents, now Pearson Education. 176pp. ISBN 0-13-353913-X.

This book combines useful real language with communicative strategies and basic work on pronunciation, stress and intonation. The material is suitable for beginners and up. Cassettes and a teacher's manual are available.

#5-40

Jazz Chants, Rhythms of American English for Students of English as a Second Language (1978) by Carolyn Graham. New York: Oxford University Press. 80pp. ISBN 0-19-502407-9. An audio cassette tape is also available.

This classic book of group 'chants,' which are spoken in chorus by the class, provides practice in pronunciation, rhythm and intonation. They are more than just a fun way to teach pronunciation, however. Students learn useful phrases and idioms from them as well. And many, such as *Banker's Wife's Blues* and *Personal Questions*, provide provocative material for discussion. Students at all levels can benefit from using these. The introduction to the book explains how to use them. AT: "My adult students love these. They often use phrases they learned from the chants months later." AS: "I've had the same response. I also really like the way these chants help students to speak up confidently."

#5-41

PD's: Pronunciation Drills in Depth, Second Edition (1983) by Edith Crowell Trager and Sara Cook Henderson. Upper Saddle River: Prentice Hall Regents, now Pearson Education. 192pp. ISBN 0-13-730920-1. Audio cassette tapes are also available.

Although the minimal pair pronunciation drills of the type presented in this book have gone out of fashion, replaced by more contextualized work, it is sometimes useful to have available short drills on specific sounds. This book provides the teacher with basic information on the English sound system, including a list of areas of difficulty for students who speak particular languages, along with drills on contrasting sounds and on intonation patterns.

#5-42

Pronouncing American English: Sounds, Stress and Intonation Second Edition (1988, 1997) by Gertrude F. Orion. Boston: Heinle & Heinle Publishers. 330pp. ISBN 0-8384-6332-0. An instructor's manual and audio cassette tapes are also available.

This is a useful book for a pronunciation or accent reduction class or for self-study. Sounds are presented contextually with diagrams to help production, dialogues for practice and listening passages for help with stress and intonation. It's best suited for high intermediate or advanced students.

#5-43

Pronunciation Pairs: An Introductory Course for Students of English (1990) by Ann Baker and Sharon Goldstein. Cambridge: Cambridge University Press. Student book is 158pp. ISBN 0-521-34972-9. A teacher's manual and audio cassette tapes are also available.

This book is intended for both classroom and independent work. It is divided into two sections: vowels and consonants, but teachers or students need not follow the sequence given. A facial diagram is given for each sound, followed by numerous exercises, some on the cassette for recognition purposes, others designed for pairwork in class. Each section ends with a note on spelling. The teacher's manual provides additional activities that help the student use the sounds in context. AT: "A clear and useable book for a pronunciation class."

See also:

Sing It! (item #4-37 in the *Activities* section). Singing is another way to learn good pronunciation, and this series provides many different kinds of songs for classroom use.

#5-44

Small Talk: More Jazz Chants (1986) by Carolyn Graham. New York: Oxford University Press. 86pp. ISBN 0-19-434220-4. Audio cassette tapes are also available.

These are shorter and easier than the *Jazz Chants* (#5-40 above) and are useful for many of the same reasons. They would be especially suitable for lower level classes. They are arranged by function (introductions, expressing likes) and have some accompanying written exercises.

#5-45

Sound Advantage: A Pronunciation Book (1992) by Stacy A. Hagen and Patricia E. Grogan. Upper Saddle River: Prentice Hall Regents, now Pearson Education. 220pp. ISBN 0-13-816190-9. Audio cassette tapes and an instructor's manual are also available.

For intermediate or advanced students, this text covers all the important aspects of English pronunciation thoroughly, yet very clearly. Listening discrimination exercises in each chapter help students understand the concepts and short production exercises give students oral practice using them. None of the material is contextualized, nor are there interactive activities here. However, at the end of each chapter students are given a paragraph to read for practice, asked to give a short oral presentation and given a photograph to describe orally. These exercises are intended to help prepare the students for oral examinations. The material is suitable for both classroom or individual work.

We can recommend this text especially for teacher reference. For example, you will find ideas on how to teach the vowel sound system which you could adapt even for lower level students. Some of the information on intonation and stress in English is important for ESL teachers to be aware of—as native speakers we aren't always conscious of how we sound.

#5-46

Sounds Great: Low-intermediate Pronunciation for Speakers of English, Book 1 (1994) by Beverly Beisbier. Boston: Heinle & Heinle Publishers. 172pp. ISBN 0-8384-3964-0. Book 2 is intermediate level. Audio cassette tapes and an instructor's manual for both books are also available.

This book for high beginners or low intermediate students focuses equally on sentence-level stress and intonation and on individual sounds. Both discrimination and production are emphasized. The authors make an effort to contextualize their exercises with family trees, calendars and directions. They also include activities for students to do in pairs. For example, to practice rising intonation there is a guessing game ("Is number one a telephone?" "No, it isn't."). This is a useful and complete textbook for classes in pronunciation. AS: "The face diagrams about making the sounds may not be helpful to students, but you can demonstrate or explain the sounds to them yourself."

Other sources of pronunciation materials:

Many of the dictionaries included in Chapter 9 have audio cassettes or CD-ROMs available which can aid students with pronunciation.

CHAPTER 6

Reading

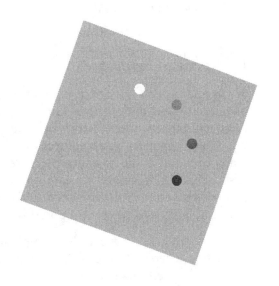

ESL classes for adults encompass all skill areas, and reading is an important one. As teachers, of course we want our students to be able to read labels, letters, bills and other kinds of basic, necessary materials. Those skills are generally included in coursebooks, as well as in the books included in the *Literacy* section. In addition to this basic reading though, we also want our students to be able to read and learn from more extended writings such as stories, books and news articles.

Content for adults

Beginning adult readers, in particular, need extended reading materials designed specifically for them. The readings need to be easy enough that students do not become discouraged, yet the content should be appropriate for and interesting to adults. (Children's books send the wrong message: 'You are a child because you do not read well.') The readings should ideally be linked to other classroom content so that they do not pose completely new topics and vocabulary. The exercises that accompany the readings should challenge the students to think about the story, not just ask them to parrot back responses.

It is also useful to have an ESL reading book for intermediate level classes as most intermediate students are not yet ready to tackle material written for native speakers. In addition, the teacher may feel more comfortable with ready-made activities and suggestions to the teacher. Teachers of advanced students may want to use newspapers, novels and other materials written for native speakers or a textbook written specifically for advanced ESL students.

Unstructured reading

In addition to classroom reading instruction, students learning English need plenty of opportunities for pleasure reading. This helps them to increase their vocabulary, improve their fluency in reading and improve their confidence in reading. It also enhances and reinforces what they have learned in their lessons. This kind of reading could be called pleasure reading, free reading, voluntary reading, leisure reading, unguided reading or fun reading. In any case the students should choose what to read themselves and decide for themselves what they are getting out of it, without a teacher-imposed structure.

Some programs have a pleasure reading library for students to borrow from. These books can be stored on a moveable cart that goes from class to class, or they could be located in a special section of a school library. Students can take some class time for free reading (for example, once a week for 20–30 minutes), or they can borrow the books to read at home. It is helpful if the books are marked according to reading level; students should be encouraged to select something they can read easily without needing to work at it. Sources for "easy readers" are listed at the end of this chapter.

Reading student writings

As you look for reading materials for your class, remember that an easy way to incorporate more reading into class activities is to have students read each others' writings. These could be stories they've written, responses to questions on a class topic, or even letters written to each other in class. (See both the *Activities* and the *Writing* sections for more ideas). If you are teaching individuals or small classes, the students can dictate their stories for you to write on paper or on the board. Those stories then become reading material.

Teacher Resources

#6-1
Headstarts: One Hundred Original Pretext Activities (1991) by Natalie Hess. Harlow, UK: Longman, now Pearson Education. 121pp. ISBN 0-582-06492-9.

In the introduction to this book the author suggests general techniques for teaching reading. The bulk of the book, however, consists of clearly described pre-reading activities that help students get the most out of all kinds of text, from newspapers to poetry to advertising. Many of the activities make use of all the language skills in working with a text, some are interactive; most are for intermediate and higher levels. Each one indicates materials needed, level, skills, time and suggested texts. The directions are clear and easy to follow.

#6-2
The Power of Reading: Insights from the Research (1993) by Stephen D. Krashen. Englewood, CO: Libraries Unlimited, Inc. 119pp. ISBN 1-56308-006-0.

In this book Krashen advocates that learners read as much as possible. While reading they don't look up vocabulary, and there is no teacher-imposed structure, except perhaps just talking about the story. Although in this book he is addressing children's reading, some of the studies he cites (here and elsewhere) suggest that adult second language learners also acquire vocabulary and make progress in English through free reading.

#6-3
Techniques and Resources in Teaching Reading (1994) by Sandra Silberstein. New York: Oxford University Press. 125pp. ISBN 0-19-434134-8.

This book contains useful techniques for teaching reading at the intermediate and advanced levels. It does not touch on literacy issues. While the focus is somewhat academic, there are parts which mention non-academic adult learners.

Student Books: Beginning Level

#6-4
Amazing Stories to Tell and Retell, Book 1 (1999) by Lynda Berish and Sandra Thibaudeau. Boston: Houghton Mifflin Company. 142pp. ISBN 0-395-88440-3.

This book contains short, true, high-interest readings organized into ten units with two related stories in each chapter. For example, a story about a family giving up TV for a year is paired with a story about *Buy Nothing Day*. Each story is preceded by an exercise and a picture to help students anticipate what it will be about. Exercises on comprehension and vocabulary follow the stories as well as discussion and retelling activities. It is suitable for high beginners.

#6-5
The Chicken Smells Good, An ESL Reader, Second Edition (1983, 1997) by William P. Pickett. Englewood Cliffs, NJ: Prentice Hall Regents, now Pearson Education. 208pp. ISBN 0-13-576216-2.

There are over 35 dialogues and stories here for beginning/high beginning students, all about people in their everyday lives. For example, we read about Kathy, who works at a medical center and is considering marrying Bob, although he drinks too much. Although the interest level is a little prosaic, the strength of these stories is the authentic speech they offer: "I'm crazy about you," for example, which is nice for beginning students to learn. Grammar is not emphasized; most of the exercises reinforce the vocabulary nicely. You could use this material to work on all skills, not just reading. *The Pizza Tastes Great* and *The Salsa is Hot* are books in the same series.

#6-6

Easy True Stories: A Picture-Based Beginning Reader (1994) by Sandra Heyer. White Plains: Longman, now Pearson Education. 91pp. ISBN 0-8013-1089-X.

These high interest stories for beginning level students are based on human interest news articles. For example, *I Think I'm Your Mother* is about a woman who is reunited with her daughter whom she had given up at birth. And *No More Housework* tells about a woman who goes on strike in order to get her family to help with housework. Each 8 to 10 paragraph story is introduced with a pre-reading picture version for students to discuss before reading the stories. The pictures do not have text written under them, but there are lines on which students can write sentences or key words.

#6-7

Facts & Figures: Basic Reading Practice, Third Edition (1980, 1999) by Patricia Ackert. Boston: Heinle & Heinle Publishers. 310pp. ISBN 0-838408-65-6. An instructor's manual and a video (with CNN clips) are also available.

This book of short nonfiction articles covers a wide range of topics, such as animals, plants, occupations and adventures. Each article is preceded by a drawing and pre-reading questions and is followed by vocabulary and content exercises. There is an audiocassette of the readings and an extensive teacher's manual. In addition, a videotape is available featuring short related stories from CNN television reports. Students enjoy learning more about the content of these stories as they read. The level of this text is suitable for high beginning adult classes; two higher-level texts in the same series are *Thoughts & Notions* and *Cause & Effect*.

See also:

Introducing the USA (item #11-6 in the *Culture* section) for beginning level cultural readings.

#6-8

My Native Land: An Anthology by New Writers (1992). New York: New Writers Voices Series, Literacy Volunteers of New York. 63 pp. ISBN 0-929631-65-X.

This is not a reading textbook in the sense of having questions or exercises before or after the reading. It is a book of short passages written by immigrants to the United States in which they tell about their own experiences. One writer, for example, tells about a festival in India, while another tells about her experience in a hurricane in Antigua. The book is easy to read and the stories are of great interest to adult learners.

#6-9

A New Beginning: An ESL Reader (1988) by Mary Mitchell Church, Keesia Harrison Hyzer and Ann Marie Niedermeier. New York: Prentice Hall Regents, now Pearson Education. 117pp. ISBN 0-13-611849-6.

This book for high beginners provides 15 readings about the experiences of an immigrant family in the U.S. Many of the events in the book are family events—a birthday, a wedding, picking up grandfather at the airport, etc. Other topics include applying for a job, getting a drivers' license and having an accident. Reading about the same characters in each story is a nice feature and lends continuity. Each chapter provides some comprehension and vocabulary exercises, discussion questions and plenty of writing topics.

#6-10
Stories for the New Millennium (1999) by David de Rocco. Virgil, Ontario: Full Blast Productions. 54pp. ISBN 1-895451-32-9.

This book contains 50 short nonfiction articles written for high beginners on a wide variety of topics, from cloning to mutual funds to food poisoning. The book is reproducible and each article and its exercises covers just one page. Some of the articles have a Canadian focus; the exercises are minimal. AT: "Reproducible reading books are rare. The price is higher than that of non-reproducible reading books because the publisher cannot expect to sell as many copies."

#6-11
Stories from the Heart: A Reading and Process Writing Book for Adults (1991) by Ronna Magy. Palatine: Linmore Publishing. 120pp. ISBN 0-916591-26-3.

The 31 stories in this book were written by adult ESL students and reflect the concerns and issues in their lives. Each one is followed by written exercises and a short composition in which the students write about their own lives. This is an inexpensive book, which adult students enjoy and learn from. The students might also be inspired by these examples to write their own stories. Students can complete some of the exercises on their own, which is useful in a multilevel class while the teacher is working with other students or as homework between classes or tutoring sessions. This book is useful for high beginners or low intermediates. A more recent book, *Beginning Stories from the Heart*, is similar but written at an even lower level.

#6-12
Stories to Tell Our Children (1992, 1996) by Gail Weinstein-Shr. Boston: Heinle & Heinle Publishers. 96pp. ISBN 0-8384-2362-0.

This low beginning reader includes fourteen wonderful short autobiographical stories told by adult English learners. One woman, for example, tells of going back to school as an older adult; another writes about escaping from Vietnam. The exercises that accompany the stories help the students expand on and personalize what they have read. AS: "I think this text would be great for an inexperienced teacher, because it provides lots of easy ways to get students talking about their experiences and impressions."

#6-13

Stories We Brought with Us: Beginning Readings, Second Edition (1986, 1994) by Carol Kasser and Ann Silverman. Englewood Cliffs: Prentice Hall Regents, now Pearson Education. 278pp. ISBN 0-13-122145-0.

This book has twenty-one simple but profound stories with universal interest, such as *The Tortoise and the Hare* and similar stories with a 'moral,' which adult students will have a lot to say about. Each story is very short and is presented at two different levels. The first version gives the story in the most basic, simple language possible; the second in more idiomatic English with more complex sentences. You could use these for two different levels of students, or you could use one as an introduction and then the other to expand the students' vocabulary and fluency. The exercises are useful; you can use them or not depending on the needs of your students. The best use of this material, though, is for retelling and discussion. AS: "My students enjoyed retelling these stories and explaining the moral in each one. I think this is because most people really like giving advice."

See also:

TOPICS *Magazine*, #12-10 in the *Internet* section, for stories and essays written by students.

#6-14

True Stories in the News: A Beginning Reader, Second Edition (1987, 1996) by Sandra Heyer. White Plains: Addison Wesley Longman, now Pearson Education. 94pp. ISBN 0-201-84660-8. An audio cassette tape is also available.

Students (and teachers) love the human interest stories in this high beginning reader. One story tells about a man who lost 400 pounds; another describes a boy who survived plunging into an icy lake. Because they are true stories, students easily identify with them. Each story is complete in itself and can be integrated into specific topics of study. Accompanying exercises check student's comprehension, improve reading skills and stimulate thought. Another book by the same author is *More True Stories* (1990), which is at a slightly higher level and also has a tape. AT: "I use the tapes before reading. Those students whose listening is good but whose literacy is weak get a start on reading the story; those whose listening is weak get extra listening practice."

#6-15

The Working Experience, 1, 2 and 3 (1991) by Jeanne H. Smith and Harry Ringel. Syracuse: New Readers Press. Book 1 is 63pp, ISBN 0-88336-965-6. A teacher's manual for the series is also available.

There is always something fascinating about true stories, even when they are written at a very low level. The students whose stories appear in this series have opinions, conflicts, memories and hopes that will certainly encourage your students to express their own ideas in response.

Each of these inexpensive readers features 15 very short stories about the work and life experiences of adult ESL students. The levels range from beginning to low intermediate. Each reading includes a photo and is followed by simple written exercises on comprehension, vocabulary practice and structure practice. Some oral exercises give students a chance to express their opinions about the story and talk about their own experiences. The teacher's manual provides useful discussion questions to be used as a pre-reading exercise before each story, and an 18-page section on teaching techniques that will be especially useful to new teachers.

Student Books: Intermediate Level

#6-16
Amazing Stories, Books 2 and 3 (1999) by Lynda Berish and Sandra Thibaudeau. Boston: Houghton Mifflin Company. Book 2 is 171pp, ISBN 0-395-88441-1 and Book 3 is ISBN 0-395-949113-0.

These stories are similar to those in Book 1 (item #6-4 above). That is, they are interesting true stories, but longer and with more complex activities. Topics include the origin of Muzak, a lost flamingo, how a power drill saved a life and other intriguing subjects.

#6-17
Building Real Life English Skills, Third Edition (1984, 1994) by Carolyn Morton Starkey and Norgina Wright Penn. Lincolnwood: NTC/Contemporary. 368pp. ISBN 0-8442-5167-4. A teacher's guide is also available.

This book is suitable for intermediate-level readers. It contains few long reading passages, but it has many short, authentic reading materials, such as employment applications and medicine labels. The teacher's guide has additional activities.

#6-18
Contact USA: Reading and Vocabulary Textbook, Third Edition (1981, 1996) by Paul Abraham and Daphne Mackey. Englewood Cliffs: Prentice Hall Regents, now Pearson Education. 256pp. ISBN 0-13-518754-0.

The readings in this book focus on different aspects of American culture such as equality, discrimination, freedom of religion, eating habits, retirement. Each page-long essay raises issues about what Americans think and do. The essays are fairly general but still provide a basis for class discussion. In many chapters there are also graphic representations (charts and graphs) relating to the topic. In the exercises, there is a strong emphasis on vocabulary development. A fairly high level of literacy is assumed. This would be appropriate for high-intermediate adult students.

#6-19

Easy English News, Elizabeth Claire, editor. P.O. Box 2596, Fair Lawn, NJ 07410. Fax: 201-791-1901. Internet: www.Elizabethclaire.com. A free sample issue is available upon request.

This tabloid-style newspaper for adult immigrants is published 10 times a year. It contains a variety of articles about topics of interest to adult ESL students, including some written by ESL students about their experiences and others about US culture. The articles are well-illustrated. Words that may be unfamiliar are set out in bold print in the articles, and a glossary page is included to explain these. The reading level is intermediate and above. AT: "One drawback of this newspaper is that it is expensive for a program to buy a subscription for each student."

#6-20

Even More True Stories, An Intermediate Reader (1992) by Sandra Heyer. White Plains, NY: Addison Wesley Longman, now Pearson Education. 96pp. ISBN 0-8013-0625-6. (A new edition is forthcoming.)

Like the other books in the *True Stories* series by the same author, this book provides highly readable human interest stories, in this case for intermediate level students. Each story is about one page long. Topics include the world's largest family, the Amish and superstitions. The accompanying exercises help students check on their comprehension and discuss their own ideas. A second edition of this book, due to be published in 2000, adds 'Challenge Pages' to every unit for students who are ready to read at a higher level.

#6-21

For Your Information, Basic Reading Skills Book 1 (1996) by Karen Blanchard and Christine Root. White Plains: Longman, now Pearson Education. 212pp. ISBN 0-201-83409-X.

This book is intended for high beginning through low intermediate students and is probably best suited to the latter. It has human interest stories that are similar in nature to the *True Stories* series (86 year old man runs in marathon, genetically modified tomatoes, etc.) but with quite a few more formal vocabulary and reading skill-building exercises included, as well as follow-up factual readings and discussion topics. The activities suggested give you plenty of ideas for practicing all of the language skills while working on this text. Low intermediate students who really want to work hard to bring their vocabulary level up could benefit a lot from this text. Books 2, 3 and 4 in the same series are also available.

See also:

Grammar in Context (item #8-12 in the *Grammar* section). Each unit is based on a short non-fiction reading, often with cultural content.

#6-22

Insights for Today, A High Beginning Reading Skills Text, Second Edition (1993, 1999) by Lorraine C. Smith and Nancy Nici Mare. Boston: Heinle & Heinle Publishers. 260pp. ISBN 0-8384-0847-8.

This is a collection of 12 readings on general interest topics such as identical twins, secondhand smoke, and the story of Alfred Nobel. Although the publisher calls the readings 'high beginning,' we think you'd be more likely to use them with low intermediate students.

Each chapter starts with some prereading questions; for example in Chapter 12 students discuss what they already know about earthquakes. A page-long reading about what causes earthquakes follows, with a flow-chart to help students organize the content. There are several exercises on vocabulary and word forms. The best part of this book, though, is the other follow-up activities. In this case, a chart that shows 16 modern earthquakes, their intensity on the Richter scale and the number of deaths each one caused. Another section shows a checklist for earthquake safety, and several discussion topics ask the students to imagine what they would do in an earthquake. Finally, a crossword puzzle reviews the new vocabulary. Another reading gives a survivor's story from the Kobe earthquake of 1995. (There are four other reading texts written by the same authors, at different levels.) AT: "This would probably work best with students who have fairly academic interests."

#6-23

Reading Workout (1994) by Jann Huizenga and Maria Thomas-Ružić. Boston: Heinle & Heinle Publishers. 166pp. ISBN 0-8384-3980-2.

Although this is described as a high beginning book, it is probably more appropriate to low-intermediate adult students. The chapters are organized by themes, such as homes, health and travel, with six different readings and related activities in each one. The readings are similar in tone to those in popular magazines—for example, there is a health quiz, a chart about different kinds of aerobic activities and how many calories they burn and a newspaper story about twin sisters over 100 years old. The content of many of the readings is human interest (*Grandma, 53, Delivers Twins*) and would be fun to discuss.

The exercises are designed to help the students focus on the main ideas and discuss their own opinions, although there are also a few vocabulary exercises to help review new words. A unique and lovely feature of this book is that it includes writings by ESL students and by immigrants at the end of each unit. Instructor's notes are provided at the back of the student book. For such a slender book, it has a lot of material and ideas.

It parallels *Writing Workout* (item #7-14) and *All Talk* by the same authors in terms of content. All three books can be used together. However, the content of *All Talk* may be less relevant to adult students than that of the other two books.

#6-24

Tales from Around the World, Stories for Whole Language Learning (1991) by Jeanne B. Becijos. San Diego, CA: Dominie Press. 88pp. ISBN 1-56270-037-5.

This book is meant for high school students, but the twelve tales it includes are authentic folk tales from many countries that adults might be just as interested in reading and discussing. Folk tales incorporate universal themes such as greed or tragic love. Most people can relate to these tales, or they can tell a similar one from their own culture.

Each tale has an introduction about the country it comes from, which is an interesting lesson in itself. The tale itself is fairly long—a dense three pages or so. The readings are followed by some questions to help get at the meaning, and creative follow-up activities are suggested.

Also look for *Festival of Folktales*, 14 more tales by the same author. ISBN 1-56270-048-0.

#6-25

Time and Space, A Basic Reader, Second Edition (1982, 1990) by Michael Connelly and Jean Sims. Englewood Cliffs, NJ: Prentice Hall Regents, now Pearson Education. 224pp. ISBN 0-13-922014-3.

This is a collection of well-written page-long articles on science topics with social relevance, such as weather, the right to die, dreams, life in space, computers and the Grand Canyon. These articles might look too advanced for intermediate students, but they are meant to be read for meaning and not studied word by word. The thoughtful topics go beyond the everyday and look at the past, present and future of the world around us. For example, *Is There Life in Space?* discusses the various ways we might discover the answer to this question. Few other ESL texts combine such sophisticated material at such a readable level.

The authors suggest that students be encouraged to read the texts quickly to develop their reading fluency and to encourage students to guess meanings of new words from context. Some comprehension exercises and scanning exercises are included in each chapter.

Student Books: Advanced Level

See also:
American Voices (item #11-2 in the *Culture* section) for advanced level biographical readings on famous Americans.

#6-26

In Context Second Edition (1982, 1996) by Jean Zukowski/Faust, Susan S. Johnston and Elizabeth E. Templin. Orlando, FL: Harcourt Brace & Co. (but available from Steck-Vaughn). 262pp. ISBN 0-8172-8794-9. An instructor's manual is also available.

This book has ten units on contemporary topics such as you might hear about on news programs. Some of the readings include: test anxiety, Mothers Against Drunk Driving, electric cars, predicting hurricanes, etc. The readings are lengthy (two pages or more) and clear but challenging. The exercises take a different approach to vocabulary learning—they ask students to find clues to the meanings of new words in the text itself. This is good training for advanced level students who will need to do more and more reading in the future. Short, structured writing exercises help to reinforce the concepts learned.

#6-27

Interactions One: A Reading Skills Book, Third Edition (1989, 1996) by Elaine Kirn and Pamela Hartmann. New York: McGraw-Hill. 259pp. ISBN 0-07-034917-7. An audio cassette tape is also available. (This book is one component in a multi-book program.)

The publisher intends this book for academic students (at a high-beginner level); however because the readings are of general interest to adult readers, and because the grammatical structures are kept fairly simple, the book would be very nice for an adult ESL learner who is at an advanced level. In other words, it's good for a pre-academic student who needs to acquire a lot more vocabulary.

The outstanding quality of this book is the very large amount of interesting reading material it contains—there is much more for students to read here than in most textbooks. The authors state that "people learn to read by reading," and this seems like a great idea. Each topic in the book has many passages in different styles: idiomatic, personal, formal and factual. For example, in the section on television there is an article on how television affects us (six paragraphs), a case study of a woman who watched too much TV (about a page), an exercise on scanning TV program guides and personal viewpoints from four different people about what TV means to them (a page and a half). There is also an interesting table of survey data about TV viewers in the U.S.

Some of the readings come with discussion questions, and there are lots of vocabulary exercises—maybe even more than your students would want to do. This book would also be useful in tutoring an advanced level student, especially one who wants to pursue further studies.

See also:

Culturally Speaking (item #5-11 in the *Speaking* section), which has high intermediate/advanced readings and discussions on North American culture.

#6-28

Reader's Choice Third Edition (1977, 1994) by E. Margaret Baudoin, et al. Ann Arbor: University of Michigan Press. 352pp. ISBN 0-472-08265-5.

This advanced reader includes a great variety of readings, from essays to advertisements, poetry and news reports. The introduction explains its focus on reading skills and gives suggestions on using the book. It gives suggestions for word study, with a section on stems and affixes and exercises on using context clues to guess meaning.

See also:
The U.S.A.: Customs and Institutions (item #11-8 in the *Culture* section) for advanced level cultural readings.

Reading for Pleasure

There are many small, inexpensive 'graded readers' available for adult new readers that might appeal to your ESL students. Unfortunately, the 'grade' level (a designation intended for mainstream students whose first language is English) of such material doesn't tell you whether it's suitable for your students because the vocabulary may still be too difficult for them.

To select books for a pleasure reading library, look first for materials intended for adults (there are a lot of these meant for teenagers). Next look for topics that really interest your students, both fiction and nonfiction. (Research, and our experience, shows that students will read challenging material if the topic is of high enough interest.) Then, decide which ones tell a good story—sometimes abridged or simplified materials are too "choppy" and even harder to understand than more advanced versions! Finally, select texts that are edited for ESL if possible; if the texts are for native speakers read through them carefully to make sure the language is accessible to your students. We find that these books average around $5 per title, so you can put together quite a varied library on a reasonably small budget.

Following are some of the readers that might be worth looking into if you are setting up a pleasure reading library. See the *Publishers* section for contact information.

Globe Fearon: They publish several series of short readers, *not* edited for ESL, including: *BesTellers®*, *Fastbacks®*, *Double Fastbacks®*, *Freedom Fighters*, *Spor-Tellers™* and *Matchbook™ Five-Minute Thrillers*. Some of these have audio cassette tapes available. **In addition, they publish *Hopes and Dreams*, a series of 20 titles about the immigrant experience.**

Heinemann Educational Publishers (titles available in the U.S. from **Delta Systems Co.**): Dozens of titles for ESL, called *Heinemann Guided Readers*, from low-beginner level through high intermediate. Some have audio cassette tapes available.

Longman (now Pearson Education): Series for ESL include: *Longman Originals* and *Longman Classics*. Some of the titles are more suitable for teenagers.

New Readers Press: Several series of readers, *not* edited for ESL, including: *Timeless Tales*, *Sundown* fiction, *Autobiography*, *Sports*, *Romance* and *Mystery*.

Oxford University Press: Several series of readers for ESL, and at several different levels, including: *Oxford Bookworms, Oxford Bookworms Factfiles* and *Storylines.*

Steck-Vaughn: Several series *not* edited for ESL, including: *The Great Series* and *Great Unsolved Mysteries.*

For more "easy readers," look in catalogs from book distributors (Chapter 13). **Miller Educational Materials** (item #13-23) has an especially large selection of these.

Other materials for pleasure reading

Trade magazines of any kind, if they capture your students' interest, are good for pleasure reading. Back issues of many magazines are often available in second hand book stores.

> AT: "My intermediate students find *Reader's Digest, Popular Science* and some women's magazines, as well as *USA Today,* to be quite readable." AS: "I've always found *National Geographic* useful, especially articles with pictures about students' home countries."

Short novels or short stories. Have your students get a public library card, take a tour together and show them where they can find books that might interest them. (If they have kids, show them where the children's section is, too!)

CHAPTER 7

Writing

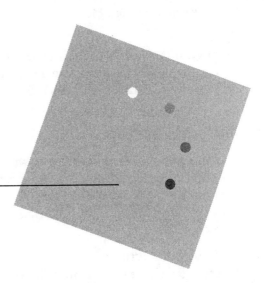

Many teachers don't realize that all levels of students, even beginners, can learn to write effectively. In fact, writing activities are an important part of every student's language learning. Writing enhances and reinforces all the other skills. We all (teachers and students) need to overcome our belief that writing must be perfect. If we put off writing until the other language skills are developed, it will be too late to develop confidence in this skill, and a major source of language reinforcement will have been neglected.

Writing enhances lessons

For literacy students, writing should be closely linked to the themes they are studying and to the language they hear, speak and read. Such writing might include labeling a picture (parts of the body, for example) or writing a variation on a model sentence or paragraph the teacher provides. (For example: "I have ___ brothers and ___ sisters.") For those who are beginning to write, copying from the board or a paper (provided that such writing has meaning for the student) is useful writing practice.

At the beginning and intermediate levels, the best way to get students involved in writing is to connect it directly with other classroom activities. Ideas, vocabulary and structures the students are using orally are recycled in another medium—the written page. This makes writing a lot less scary, and gives the students more confidence.

Group writing as well as individual writing is a productive use of class time. Starting with picture cues, students can work in small groups to compose a story. In the process of working together, students negotiate the style and sequence of the story. If the stories are written on large poster paper or 'cling' sheets (pads of these reusable plastic sheets are available from business supply stores; they stick to the wall with static electricity) the whole class can read the finished products.

Start with meaning

Some good ideas for starting to write can be found in the 'process writing approach,' in which students focus on meaning first and on editing last, and in some 'cooperative learning' activities in which students help each other to write or to generate ideas. Many of the materials we recommend in this chapter incorporate these concepts.

Some other writing texts you will find (especially the more academic ones) dissect the writing process into discrete skills and elements to be learned separately. For beginners and for pre-academic students in general, we think you want to avoid this as it takes the student too far away from the meaning of the writing. It is better to focus on communicating as the primary goal.

Finally, writing can and should be a lot of fun. First and foremost, look for materials and topics your students will enjoy and want to write about.

Teacher Resources

#7-1

Techniques in Teaching Writing (1983) by Ann Raimes. New York: Oxford University Press. 164pp. ISBN 0-19-434131-3.

> This practical guide to non-academic writing shows the teacher how to integrate writing into the ESL class. It provides background information on various approaches to teaching writing as well as how to encourage writing through pictures, reading, interviewing and listening. It also has a useful section on ways teachers can respond to student writing.

#7-2

Think, Write, Share: Process Writing for Adult ESL and Basic Education Students (1994) by Joyce Scane, Anne Marie Guy and Lauren Wenstrom. San Diego: Dominie Press, Inc. 86pp. ISBN 1-56270-108-8.

> This teacher's reference gives some really practical ideas and examples on helping adult students to work cooperatively on their writing. For example, there is quite a detailed section on brainstorming, with several different types explained and demonstrated; another section on peer conferencing gives plenty of rationale on this technique and tips on how to make it successful. The authors are writing directly out of their classroom experience, so the examples are concrete and useful. There's a good chapter on using computers for writ-

ing, and some ready-to-use teaching activities at the end of the book. Most other resources on process writing are about teaching kids, so this one focusing on adults is a gem.

#7-3

Write After: Group Projects as Pre-Writing Activities (1993) by Heather McKay and Abigail Tom. Englewood Cliffs: Prentice Hall. 106pp. ISBN 0-13-042763-2. (This book has now gone out of print but may be found in libraries and resource centers.)

This is a reproducible teacher resource book organized around six topics that are of interest to adults: cultural adaptation, work, language learning, relationships, education and media/ TV. Within each topic there are six activities, designed to provoke discussion among students, followed by related writing topics. In the work chapter, for example, students define work, consider their own interests and skills related to work and do individual research on possible jobs. Some of the activities are appropriate for high beginners, but most are more suitable for intermediate and advanced students.

#7-4

Writing Our Lives: Reflections on Dialogue Journal Writing with Adults Learning English (1991, 1996), Joy Kreeft Peyton and Jana Staton, editors. McHenry, IL: Delta Systems Co. and the Center for Applied Linguistics. 149pp. ISBN 0-937354-71-6.

This is a very interesting and thought-provoking set of articles for those who would like to try using dialogue journals in adult ESL classes. The articles are based on personal experience and include practical suggestions for teachers at all levels, including beginners. There are many good ideas here for integrating dialogue journals with all aspects of language learning, not just writing. There is an extensive resource list at the end for further information and research about using this technique with different audiences, including adults, deaf and hard of hearing students, teacher trainees, young children and students with special needs.

#7-5

Writing Warmups: 70 Activities for Prewriting (1989, 1999) by Heather McKay and Abigail Tom. San Francisco: Alta Book Center Publishers. 120pp. ISBN 1-882483-74-X.

This is a reproducible teacher resource book of oral activities, designed to help students think about specific aspects of writing such as audience, point of view and classification. In the point of view chapter, for example, students identify family members based on their statements, they do a roleplay of people discussing a problem, and they survey classmates on television and violence. Most of the activities are short and require little preparation. Some of them are appropriate for high beginners but most are better for higher levels. At the end of each chapter, there is a list of composition topics.

Student Materials

#7-6

Drawing on Experience: The Fundamentals of Good Writing (1996) by John Dumicich and Christine Root. New York: McGraw-Hill, Inc. 141pp. ISBN 0-07-018022-9.

To help students develop their ideas, these authors have students draw an illustration first, then write about it. For example, in Chapter 6 about money, students first discuss their own attitudes about money and talk about some expressions, like "money doesn't grow on trees." Then they are asked to draw a picture of what they would do with $1000. Following this is a three-stage process to begin writing, and several revising and editing steps. Other topics include: flag, travel, food, dream and peace.

The book is best suited for intermediate or high intermediate students but this technique could be adapted to any level. (See *Drawing Out*, item #4-4 in the *Activities* section for further ideas on using this technique with beginners.)

#7-7

From Writing to Composing: An Introductory Composition Course for Students of English (1988) by Beverly Ingram and Carol King. Cambridge: Cambridge University Press. Student book is 128pp., ISBN 0-521-37938-5. A teacher's manual is also available.

This is a well-organized writing book for intermediate students. Students work on a variety of structured exercises that help them gain writing skills. For example, in one section students write a short dictation about Thomas Edison's working day. Then they answer a few questions and discuss Edison and other inventors. Next they rewrite the paragraph, adding several phrases to expand the passage. They make their own cloze exercise by omitting every 5th word and practice this, then another dictation follows. This leads to an exercise on sentence fragments and clauses. Later students write several short compositions about their own daily routine. Throughout the book, students are introduced to correction symbols and given plenty of practice with these. We think it is good that they learn how to use these.

The book has a very well developed teacher's manual which explains the why and how of teaching writing as a process and provides additional activities for each unit. You'll want the teacher's manual in order to use this material most effectively. AS: "Although this is a very nice book, you can do many of the same things using *10 Steps* (item #7-12, below)."

#7-8

The Multicultural Workshop: A Reading and Writing Program, Books 1, 2 and 3 (1994-1995) by Linda Lonan Blanton and Linda Lee. Boston: Heinle & Heinle Publishers. Book 1 is 194pp, ISBN 0-8384-4834-8. A 'reading box' (100 cards with supplemental readings) is also available.

Book 1 of this series is suitable for intermediate adult students and Book 2 for advanced. This book uses articles and discussions on cross-cultural topics as the basis for writing, and takes the classroom workshop approach to getting students started in the writing process. For example, one story by an immigrant recalls the process of coming from Russia to America as a young girl. The students read and discuss this, then write about the surprises and difficulties they may have faced in coming here. Some of the readings are folktales with universal themes. Suggested exercises sometimes ask students to write about a story from the point of view of one of the characters. Others have students write about their own observations and experiences, then share these with other students. Journal writing is integrated into each chapter. The reading box provides additional multilevel readings on related topics. Book 2 seems richer in content than Book 1, but both deal with similar themes, including personal identification, relationships and making choices.

See also:
Picture Stories (item #5-15 in the *Speaking and Listening* section) and *More Picture Stories* for picture sequences that lend themselves to writing activities, especially for group writing.

#7-9
Put It in Writing, Second Edition (1981, 1988) by David Blot and David M. Davidson. Boston: Heinle & Heinle Publishers. 124pp. ISBN 0-8384-2941-6.

For intermediate students, this book supplies some interesting starting points to stimulate their writing. We especially like the 'story completion' activity. For example, students see a photograph and read a story about a man who ran out of gas on a dark, cold night, then they finish the story. The topics are interesting (many of them are about immigrants) and open-ended. The book also supplies some content questions to start your students thinking; there are no structure exercises.

#7-10
Reflection and Beyond: Expanding Written Communication (1993) by Laurie Blass and Meredith Pike-Baky. Boston: Heinle & Heinle Publishers. 136pp. ISBN 0-8384-2305-1. An instructor's manual and audio cassette tape are also available.

The publisher intends this book for an academic low-intermediate level; however the content is not really academic at all and the material would be very useful for an advanced level adult ESL student, especially one who plans on further study and needs to develop more confidence in writing.

This book gives students an opportunity to think about a topic in detail (for example, think about a person you admire), develop vocabulary about it (adjectives and expressions for describing a person), read one or two sample writings on the topic (a poem about someone's mother and an essay about a baseball coach), brainstorm their own ideas and develop them in writing. Suggestions are included for student-to-student feedback on the writing exercises. There are also photos for discussion stimulus. The topics are refreshingly different from many other texts, including *Music as Personal History*, *Future Gadgets* and *Saving the Planet*.

#7-11

Share Your Paragraph, An Interactive Approach to Writing, Second Edition (1987, 1999) by George M. Rooks. Upper Saddle River: Prentice Hall Regents, now Pearson Education. 180pp. ISBN 0-13-660796-9. A teacher's guide is also available.

This book is written for high beginning to low intermediate students, but even more advanced students would benefit from the process of writing as it is presented here. There are twenty units, each of them based on an interesting paragraph. Many of these are by and about ESL students, and are presented with an intriguing photograph. For example, Paragraph 10 is "Write about your classmate's best childhood friend," and the example paragraph is about a woman from Iran who still writes to her friend from kindergarten. The students read and discuss the paragraph and practice some of the structures. Then they interview a classmate, take notes and write a paragraph about the classmate's childhood friend. Next, they discuss the paragraph together and make changes to improve it.

Some careful editing exercises are provided, such as using pronouns, punctuation, articles, etc. In all there are four to five hours of classroom work in each unit. We think the real value of this book, though, is that the students are writing to communicate.

#7-12

10 Steps: Controlled Composition for Beginning and Intermediate Language Development, Third Edition (1974, 1996) by Gay Brookes and Jean Withrow. Upper Saddle River: Prentice Hall Regents, now Pearson Education. 60pp. ISBN 0-13-456989-X.

Originally published in 1974, this text is still very useful for careful structure practice. The book is not intended to provide communication activities, but instead allows students to focus on accuracy and form. For example, students are given a brief (eleven sentences) selection about a woman who owns many cats. They are asked to rewrite the entire passage, changing the person to a man instead. This means they will pay close attention to the pronouns as they write. Other exercises instruct the students to change the tense or combine sentences.

This technique is especially useful for 'false beginners,' or for students who speak fairly well but whose writing is inaccurate or lags behind the level of their speaking. The book has 58 such passages; they make great homework assignments. *26 Steps*, with similar exercises at a much higher level, is also available. AS: "I've seen this technique work well with a student who had entrenched language patterns that oral correction couldn't help." AT: "I have some reservations about this way of teaching writing. I'm not sure that the result is any better than having a student do a page of grammar exercises."

#7-13
Write from the Start, Second Edition (1984, 1994) by David M. Davidson and David Blot. Boston: Heinle & Heinle Publishers. 135pp. 0-8384-4848-8.

This writing book for high beginners starts with students talking about a topic before writing about it. At the beginning of the book models are provided for writing about a topic, which students may use if they choose. The topics are interesting to adults and are mostly stories about people (classmates, holidays, everyday events and family dilemmas). One section of the book has photographs that students discuss and then write about; they have to invent a story that explains the picture. The last 50 pages provide structure exercises, such as pronoun practice, each in the context of a new story. *Put It in Writing* (#7-9 above) is an intermediate level book by the same authors.

#7-14
Writing Workout: A Program for New Students of English (1990) by Jann Huizenga and Maria Thomas-Ružić. Boston: Heinle & Heinle Publishers. 186pp. ISBN 0-8384-3960-8.

This book is appropriate for intermediate or advanced adult students. Students begin by talking about a topic, generate vocabulary, work on related oral activities with a partner and then write. The writing topics are quite interesting and there is a good range in the types of writing. For example, in a section about household appliances, students imagine there is an electrical power shortage and they have to decide which three appliances are the most important to them, and explain this in writing. In a further section on purchasing things, students write a short classified ad, based on examples in the text. Another assignment has students writing a short letter of inquiry to a computer company. Some exercises for structure practice are provided. A grammar appendix is provided so that students can look up their individual problems. There is also an appendix called an 'Activity Bank' of additional writing activities.

Because the sections of the book are nicely interconnected, this would be most effective if used in a class where there is regular attendance. (Related titles, *Reading Workout* and *All Talk* are written by the same authors and are based on the same themes—home, family, health, travel, etc.)

Other sources for writing ideas

Pictures and photos that are interesting and evocative can provide a stimulus for writing. Ask your library if they have a picture/artwork file.

Use readings, especially ones about student experiences, as a starting point.

Letter and journal writing (student to student, student to teacher, etc.) are good ways to practice writing to communicate.

See also:
The *Activities* section (in Chapter 4) for many classroom exercises that incorporate writing.

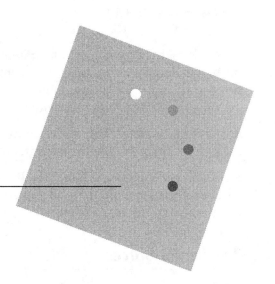

Grammar

odern language teaching recognizes that knowing grammar does not actually give you a handle on speaking the language, and so the formal study of grammar has taken a smaller role in the classroom than in the past. This is especially true in adult ESL, where communication is the main goal for many students. Nonetheless, teaching some grammar is still important for the following reasons:

1. Patterns—Grammar rules sometimes do explain why we say things the way we do in English. That is, a rule can describe a pattern that makes sense out of what otherwise looks like confusion. An experienced teacher has short grammar lessons ready for teaching grammar points as they come up, which is when the students are most likely to connect the rule with real language. Another effective strategy is to bring in a short grammar lesson you've prepared based on some of the students' statements or writings of the day before.

2. Expectations—Many students, especially if they have some educational background from their home country, expect to learn grammar. If they don't see grammar lessons included in the course, they may feel the course is not rigorous enough, or that they aren't really learning anything. In this case, the teacher who would prefer not to teach much formal grammar may have to compromise so that the students are getting at least some of what they expect.

3. Tests—Correct grammar usage is measurable, and for that reason grammar is often a central part of tests students have to take. If your students' goals are academic (they would like to enroll in college someday or take an advanced training course) you might want to incorporate more formal grammar into their lessons. This is not as necessary if the students' goals are primarily communication.

We have tried to select those grammar books that offer the most context and the most interactive methods for presenting the material. In the case of grammar, some of the most useful and interesting books are the teacher references. These provide you with grammar activities that you can pull out when needed.

AS: "I have to admit, I've always enjoyed teaching grammar. It's like giving the students a tool to play with and watching what they can construct with it."

AT: "For me, grammar is like a pit. If you start there, you never get out. There's always something more to be explained and examined. On the other hand, if it is integrated into the rest of the course content, it is very useful."

Teacher Resources

#8-1
Creative Questions: Lively Uses of the Interrogative (1995) by Natalie Hess and Laurel Pollard. Harlow: Longman, now Pearson Education. 104pp. ISBN 0-582-0895-81.

This book has dozens of useful ideas you can use to get your students practicing questions. Many of these are fun, interactive activities that will give practice with more than just grammar. For example, 'Review Circles' is an exercise in which each student writes two or three questions about material they have recently studied. Students sit opposite each other in two circles and take turns asking the questions, then they change partners and repeat. Most of the activities are suited to intermediate students, but could be adapted up or down if needed.

See also:
The ESL Miscellany (item #9-20 in the *Vocabulary* section), which has a 50-page chapter of grammar lists. These would be useful either for teacher reference or student use (beginning through intermediate levels; they may also be useful as review material for advanced students).

#8-2
The Grammar Book: An ESL/EFL Teacher's Course (1983) by Marianne Celce-Murcia and Diane Larsen-Freeman. Rowley: Heinle & Heinle Publishers. 655pp. ISBN 0-8384-2850-9.

This lengthy reference grammar may tell more than most teachers want to know. However, it may be the best place to read about difficult topics, such as article usage, in order to understand them thoroughly yourself. The book is clearly indexed by words and topics and contains teaching suggestions for each grammar area.

#8-3

Grammar Chants: More Jazz Chants (1993), by Carolyn Graham. New York: Oxford University Press. 98pp. ISBN 0-19-434236-0. An audio cassette tape is also available.

You can select one of these simple, short chants to illustrate a particular structure your students are learning. For example, try 'He Loves the Ocean' to practice the third person singular *-s*. These chants provide good oral practice of grammatical structures although they lack the "bite" (both in humor and in content) of the original *Jazz Chants* (see item #5-40). Primarily for beginning through low intermediate level students.

#8-4

Grammar Games: Cognitive, Affective and Drama Activities for EFL students (1984) by Mario Rinvolucri. Cambridge: Cambridge University Press. 138pp. ISBN 0-521-27773-6.

This photocopiable resource book contains imaginative games for grammar practice. Some of them are adapted from familiar games, such as *Dominoes* or *Snakes and Ladders*. Others are very unusual and require that the teacher be willing to take risks. (The spelling and some of the vocabulary in the book is British.) A second book, *More Grammar Games* by Paul Davis and Mario Rinvolucri is also available. AT: "I love the time game in which students move around a board and tell what they (or someone else) does at a particular time. There are also nice suggestions about working with grammar errors."

#8-5

Grammar Practice Activities: A Practical Guide for Teachers (1988) by Penny Ur. Cambridge: Cambridge University Press. 288pp. ISBN 0-521-33847-6.

The introduction to this book describes the role of practice activities in grammar learning. The remainder of the book includes a great variety of short, easy-to-use communicative activities for practicing grammar. They're arranged by grammar points and often include more than one content area (i.e., food, airplanes or weather) in one activity. Some activities include visuals which may be photocopied. For example, to practice possessives there is a family tree which students can use to define relationships; i.e., "Jack is Tom's uncle." There are also plenty of ideas for expanding and creating your own activities.

#8-6

Practical English Usage, Second Edition (1981, 1995) by Michael Swan. Oxford: Oxford University Press. 658pp. ISBN 0-19-431197-X.

This is a useful desk reference for the teacher who occasionally needs to check on something that comes up in class. For example, the phrases *as if* and *as though*: do they mean the same? Do we use a past tense or present tense form after them? This reference gives you the answers quickly and clearly. Both British and American usages are discussed.

#8-7

Teaching and Learning Grammar (1987) by Jeremy Harmer. New York: Longman, now Pearson Education. 71pp. ISBN 0-582-74623-X.

This brief book helps the teacher integrate the study of grammar with a communicative curriculum. The short theoretical sections include tasks and exercises for the reader, which are very helpful in applying the information to the teacher's own practice. In addition, there are specific activities for presenting and practicing grammar, such as using interviews to practice the past tense. We especially like the short chapter called *Discovery Techniques*, which clearly shows how you can lead students to discover grammar rules themselves from short reading passages.

#8-8

Techniques and Resources in Teaching Grammar (1988) by Marianne Celce-Murcia and Sharon L. Hilles. New York: Oxford University Press. 189pp. ISBN 0-19-434191-7.

This book contains good suggestions for organizing a grammar lesson as well as specific activities. These can be adapted to your own classes but are not presented in ready-to-use form. We especially like the chapter on using graphics, which includes ideas on using charts, tables, schedules, graphs and other information grids to create discussion and grammar lessons. The book is most appropriate for higher level classes.

Student Materials

#8-9

Beginning Interactive Grammar: Activities and Exercises (1993) by Irene S. McKay. Boston: Heinle & Heinle Publishers. 282pp. ISBN 0-8384-3926-8. An instructor's manual is also available.

If your high beginning students need grammar practice and your program has irregular attendance or you lack the budget for a full-fledged program like *Focus on Grammar* (#8-10 below), this book is a nice choice. It introduces each grammar point with a story. For example, the past tense of *be* is introduced with a story about last Thanksgiving (all the banks and offices were closed, etc.). Then students interview each other about the last holiday they celebrated. Several more interview activities follow, in which students gather information from the other students in the class. Then some writing activities give students a chance to practice the forms again. Because they are writing and speaking about themselves and each other, the activities remain interesting and adaptable to varying levels. Each lesson also includes a page of grammar explanation for study. This is a simple but useful text.

#8-10

Focus on Grammar: A Basic Course for Reference and Practice (1994) by Irene E. Schoenberg. New York: Addison Wesley Longman, now Pearson Education. Student book is 462pp. ISBN 0-201-65681-7. Workbook, audio cassette tapes, teacher's manual and an interactive software program on CD-ROM are also available. (A new edition has since been published, which we have not yet reviewed.)

Numerous teachers have told us that they and their students like this series. This one is best suited for high-beginning level students, or beginners if they are quite literate in their own language. Each grammar concept is presented first with an amusing conversation accompanied by a charming cartoon. For example, in a unit about the past tense of *be* a man phones his elderly mother and discovers she's been dating a younger man—"Mom, where were you last night?" Some comprehension questions follow. Next, the grammar forms are presented in a series of charts. Many practice exercises help the students to practice the forms in writing and some interesting communicative activities give them a chance to use the grammar on their own. (By the way, the story about the elderly mother has a surprise ending.) There is more extensive practice here for each grammar point than in any other book we know about. Each unit has a self-test with answers in the back of the book. There are also nice appendixes of grammar rules and other information.

#8-11

Focus on Grammar: An Intermediate Course for Reference and Practice (1994) by Marjorie Fuchs and Miriam Westheimer with Margaret Bonner. New York: Addison Wesley Longman, now Pearson Education. Student book is 345pp. ISBN 0-201-65685-X. Workbook, audio cassette tapes, teacher's manual and an interactive software program on CD-ROM are also available. (A new edition has since been published, which we have not yet reviewed.)

This intermediate grammar text is similar to the Basic Course in the series (see previous title) but with less extensive exercises and with somewhat more focus on grammar rules. The material is interesting; for example the unit on the past continuous starts with the police interviewing a burglary suspect ("What were you doing between 7:00 and 9:00?"). Like the Basic text, interesting communicative activities help the students to practice the structures. For example, they describe an automobile accident based on some pictures; they take turns questioning a suspect in court. Some of the activities in this book are especially clever and the topics are interesting and relevant to adults; they are a bit more serious in tone than in the first volume.

A high-intermediate and an advanced level are also available; we didn't review these. All the books in this series are best suited to courses with regular attendance, as some continuity is needed.

#8-12

Grammar in Context Second Edition (1986, 1996), Books 1, 2 and 3 by Sandra Elbaum. Heinle & Heinle Publishers. Book 1 is 320pp., ISBN 0-8384-4688-4. An instructor's manual is available for each level.

Although its new format is not very appealing, this book is still a gem. Each grammar point is illustrated with a paragraph of high interest to immigrant students. For example, to teach comparatives there is a reading on auto insurance: ". . . insurance rates for married men are *lower than* for unmarried men. Statistics show that married men have *fewer* accidents." This is followed by numerous practice exercises that give the students a chance to use comparisons. (There are thorough language notes for each structure but this may be too much information for non-academic students.) Teacher's manuals are also available. The series is suitable for high beginning through intermediate students, and you'll find the material is quite adaptable to your students' needs, as you can elect to do more or less of the supplementary exercises. AS: "My students were really interested in the short readings. We used them for discussion, dictation, made computer games out of them and many other language activities."

#8-13

GrammarWork, Second Edition (1982, 1996) Books 1, 2, 3, and 4 by Pamela Peterson Breyer. Upper Saddle River: Prentice Hall Regents, now Pearson Education. Each book is 160pp. Book 1 is ISBN 0-13-340241-X.

This workbook-style series has been around since 1982 and is one of the most useful sources for simple, straightforward grammar practice of one grammar structure at a time. Each short exercise starts with an example that demonstrates the structure in a context, followed by a dozen or so practice sentences, all on the same topic. For example, an exercise about using *for* and *since* is called "She's been talking on the telephone for a half hour," and has fill-in-the-blank sentences about people in an office. The students can do these orally or in writing. The material can be taught in sequence, or any exercise can just be used as needed—the four books cover beginning through high intermediate levels. An answer key in the back gives students the option of correcting their own work.

AS: "I've used these as extra work for students who finished their other assignments early."

#8-14

The New Grammar in Action (1998), Books 1, 2 and 3 by Barbara H. Foley and Elizabeth R. Neblett. Boston: Heinle & Heinle Publishers. Each book is 198pp. Book 1 is ISBN 0-8384-6719-9. Audio cassette tapes are available for each level (tapescripts appear in the back of the student books).

Has it ever occurred to you that most grammar study involves primarily reading and writing? This grammar series is unique in that the focus is much more on listening and speaking; not surprising since one of the authors, Barbara

Foley, has written several great listening texts as well. Each grammar structure is presented in an interesting context (for example, *can/can't* in a chapter on weather—what you can or can't do in each climate; past tense regular verbs are presented in a story about moving to a new apartment—they looked, rented, painted, etc.). Several listening activities accompanied by simple drawings, photos or charts introduce the students to the structure. Some short written exercises review the structure, then students are given questions or an interview to practice it themselves. Finally, some short writing exercises follow to practice the same grammar structure. The topics all have a modern feel and will be of interest to adults. The students get plenty of opportunities to share their ideas. The levels range from high beginning through intermediate. The work progresses in little steps and doesn't seem too challenging or overwhelming.

#8-15
Real-Life English Grammar, **Books 1, 2, 3 and 4 (1991) by Richard Firsten (Books 1&4), and Susan Kanter (Books 2&3). Austin: Steck-Vaughn Company. Each book is 61pp. Book 1 is ISBN 0-8114-4625-5. Teacher's editions are available for each level.**

This inexpensive, work-book style grammar series correlates with the *Real-Life English* coursebooks (see item #2-5), but could easily be used by itself for grammar instruction. The level ranges from low-beginning through intermediate and each book has 10 chapters with about six pages of exercises in each chapter. We think that students will like working with these texts because they are not overwhelming, yet the topics are interesting. The best aspect of this book is that each grammar point is presented in authentic contexts in which native speakers really use the grammar. For example, past continuous—what were people doing on July 20, 1969 when astronauts landed on the moon? Or, past tense questions—a shopping mall survey asking, "Why did you come to the mall today?" This is sensible instruction that doesn't teach students more than they need to know. For grammar reinforcement, these little books are a 'best buy'—you get lots of good teaching ideas for the money.

See also:
Share Your Paragraph **(item #7-11 in the *Writing* chapter), in which structure exercises are integrated into communicative writing activities.**

10 Steps: Controlled Composition **(item #7-12 in the *Writing* chapter), which gives students practice with grammar structures in the context of re-writing a paragraph.**

#8-16

Understanding and Using English Grammar, **Third Edition (1981, 1999) by Betty Schrampfer Azar. Upper Saddle River: Prentice Hall Regents, now Pearson Education. 496pp. ISBN 0-13-958661-X. A teacher's guide, workbook and transparencies are also available.** *Note: This is the blue book.*

This very popular upper level grammar book is a useful resource for teachers and students. The grammar explanations are very clear. However, the practice exercises are less useful as they lack context and coherence; that is, the topics change from one sentence to the next. Students preparing for the TOEFL test find it useful. The lower level books in the same series are *Basic English Grammar* (red book; lowest level in series) and *Fundamentals of English Grammar* (black book; intermediate level). An interactive software program on CD-ROM (*Azar Interactive*) is also available; we haven't reviewed this.

Other grammar resources:

Many learner's dictionaries, like the *Longman Dictionary of American English for Learners* (item #9-8), have nice concise grammar explanation sections with exercises for the students to work on.

See also the *Coursebooks* section (Chapter 2), as many of these texts integrate grammar lessons into the rest of the course work.

CHAPTER 9

Dictionaries and Vocabulary

Words are clearly the basic building blocks of a language, but how they are accessed (through dictionaries or other reference works) and how they are taught (by means of vocabulary lists or in context, for example) has differed over time.

Pros and cons

Among ESL teachers, there is considerable controversy over the use of dictionaries. Many students arrive in ESL classes so wedded to bilingual electronic or print dictionaries that they are unable to listen or read without constantly thumbing through them. Some teachers do not find this to be a problem, but others feel that this kind of dependence reduces the student's ability to reach a kind of global understanding of content and to guess at meaning from context. The student becomes so concerned about each individual word that he or she is unable to follow what is going on in class. Furthermore, a small electronic or print dictionary frequently misleads its user by giving only one or two synonyms, which may not include the meaning being sought.

At the same time, a dictionary can provide a student with key help at important moments, particularly when a new term or concept has been introduced. Students who learn to use a dictionary well gain a skill that can help them to become independent learners.

Working with words

In the *Dictionaries* sections of this chapter, we have included learners' dictionaries at various levels, starting with picture dictionaries for beginners and going on to text dictionaries, which are appropriate for intermediate and advanced students.

We think that students should start using a monolingual (English/English) dictionary early in their language learning process. A dictionary is a complex tool, though, so beginning and intermediate students will need a lot of help and encouragement from the instructor as well as time to get used to the process of using one. You don't want students getting frustrated however, so encourage them to use a picture dictionary if they're not ready for a text dictionary yet. Of course, when they need them, students still can (and will) use bilingual dictionaries.

The *Vocabulary* section of this chapter includes books with ideas and materials for teaching and reinforcing vocabulary. It is our belief that vocabulary is best learned in a context rather than through unrelated word lists. Students should learn vocabulary from what they read and hear.

The final section, *Idioms*, offers some resources for teaching and learning those trickiest of vocabulary items.

Picture Dictionaries

#9-1

Basic Oxford Picture Dictionary (1994) by Margot F. Gramer. New York: Oxford University Press. The monolingual English edition is 120pp, ISBN 0-19-434468-1. A teacher's resource book, audio cassette tapes, workbook, transparencies and wall charts are also available. *(Note: This one has a red cover.)*

This is a very clearly illustrated and useful dictionary for beginners. It illustrates 1200 words of basic vocabulary, organized thematically (food, clothing, housing). It is especially suitable for low beginners and beginners, because there are fewer words per page than in other picture dictionaries, and the pictures are less complex. The book is easy for students to learn to use.

In addition to depicting objects and parts, the dictionary also has many pictures of people doing things (slicing, chopping, running) and includes a few picture sequences (steps in doing the laundry). The *Teacher's Resource Book* contains detailed suggestions for using the dictionary as well as reproducible worksheets. A workbook provides additional practice. In addition there are picture cards, wall charts (posters), transparencies and cassettes. The accompanying *Basic Oxford Picture Dictionary Literacy Program* (see #3-4 in the *Literacy* section), though expensive, is an excellent all-in-one program for new readers. The dictionary is available in monolingual or bilingual (in a variety of languages) editions. It is inexpensive enough that students can buy their own copies.

#9-2

Longman Photo Dictionary (1987) by Marilyn S. Rosenthal and Daniel B. Freeman. White Plains: Longman, now Pearson Education. 91pp. ISBN 0-8013-0004-5. (A teacher's guide, three workbooks, an audio cassette tape and bilingual editions in Chinese, Spanish and Korean are also available.)

The color photos in this dictionary are arranged by category (food, animals, doctor, etc.) and each page has a suggested mini-practice (a short question/answer exercise). The vocabulary and topics are suitable for beginning through low intermediate students. Some of the pictures are excellent, very clear and explicit, others are a bit fuzzy and small, especially for 'over 40' eyes. Clothing, for example, is very easy to use, while the food pictures are small and might not be recognizable if you did not already know the word. The labels are occasionally unclear. The index is easy to use and is helpful in finding an illustration quickly.

#9-3

The New Oxford Picture Dictionary (1988) by E. C. Parnwell. New York: Oxford University Press. The monolingual English edition is 124pp, ISBN 0-19-434199-2. Bilingual editions are available in nine different languages. Workbooks, transparencies, wall charts and a teacher's guide are also available. *(Note: This one has a blue cover.)*

This is an excellent picture dictionary for high beginning students. It illustrates 2400 words, and the pictures and vocabulary are slightly more complex and detailed than those in the *Basic OPD* (#9-1). They are also organized thematically (postal system, highway travel, sports). A workbook and an activity book with an accompanying cassette give students additional practice. Overhead transparencies and wall charts showing each page of the dictionary are also available as well as vocabulary playing cards. This book is a popular classroom tool, probably because much of the information is what students want to know, and they can use it on their own to some extent.

#9-4

The New Oxford Picture Dictionary CD-ROM Monolingual edition (1997). New York: Oxford University Press. *Software is Windows and Mac compatible.* ISBN 0-19-458866-1.

This is an easy-to-use vocabulary tool (based on the *NOPD*, #9-3 above) that talks to you! Your students can click on any item in a picture and hear and read the word that identifies it. Beyond that, there are many different kinds of exercises to try so students can test their own knowledge. For example, see a word, click on the right picture and hear the happy chime. Or, hear the word and find the right picture. Or, see a picture and select the right word. If this sounds confusing, it really isn't—once you try it you'll see it's self-explanatory. There are other features as well, including stories and dialogues.

We think what's nice about this program is that students can direct their own practice. There are options for learning with different kinds of input—listening, reading or identifying pictures—and these reinforce each other nicely. This is very useful for beginning through low intermediate students, and not overwhelming. AT: "I had a little trouble figuring out how to use it. I also felt the dialogues and stories were aimed more at adolescents than at adults. Most of the pictures were clear but a few were identifiable only if the word was already known."

#9-5

The Oxford Picture Dictionary, Monolingual edition (1998), by Norma Shapiro and Jayme Adelson-Goldstein. New York: Oxford University Press. 208pp. ISBN 0-19-470059-3. Bilingual editions in at least 10 languages are available, which might be useful for the students' self-study and home reference. Also available are: workbooks at three levels, teacher's book, audio cassette tapes, overhead transparencies; and a website, www.picturedictionary.org. *(Note: this book has a black cover.)*

This large format book is the 'Cadillac' of the picture dictionaries! It illustrates over 3,700 words arranged in 140 different topics. The drawings are colorful and detailed and include scenarios from every imaginable aspect of life in the real world. Of particular interest might be the sections on cars and car maintenance, jobs and job skills, and health care. The section on community is especially good and includes scenes about crime, public safety and emergencies. Each page has a short practice exercise. The teacher's book offers a lot of suggestions for making interactive lessons about each topic.

There is a lot of vocabulary here that adult students need to know; however, the book may seem overwhelming to beginning level students (they should start with the *Basic OPD,* item #9-1, reviewed above). Every intermediate ESL classroom should have a set of these.

Text Dictionaries

How do you select the best text dictionary for your students? A dictionary should be a help, not a hindrance, so the most important thing is to find one that will not be frustrating for them to use. To compare several dictionaries, choose a few test words and read the definitions for the same words in each dictionary. Which entries would give your students the kind of information they need, in the way they can best understand it? (For example, we looked at entries for *race* and *verdict* to help evaluate these dictionaries.)

Of the dictionaries below, the one we are most familiar with is the *Longman Dictionary of American English* (#9-8). When writing descriptions of the other dictionaries we considered this our baseline for comparison.

The following dictionaries are presented in order of their level and complexity, starting with the lower levels.

#9-6

Everyday American English Dictionary: A Basic Dictionary for English Language Learning (1996) by Richard Spears, editor. Chicago: NTC/Contemporary. 389pp. ISBN 0-8325-0337-1.

This is a small, portable-sized low cost student dictionary that has only 5,500 basic words. It is designed 'not to overwhelm the user,' so each entry has only a pronunciation guide and a definition. Most of the definitions are clear. Alternate word forms are not given, and very few examples are included. It also does not include two-word verbs or common alternate meanings of words. The dictionary might be appropriate for high beginning through intermediate level students, though because of its limitations, it may not be the dictionary they will need as they become more proficient.

#9-7

Beginner's Dictionary of American English Usage (1986, 1995) by P. H. Collin, Miriam Lowi and Carol Weiland. Chicago: NTC/Contemporary. 279pp. ISBN 0-8442-0439-0.

This is another portable-sized low cost student dictionary of interest to high beginning through intermediate students. Although it has only 4,000 entries it is in many ways more useful than the previous dictionary. Each entry has a brief definition and one or more examples to make the meaning clear. The parts of speech are written out and so are easy to identify; alternate forms are given for many verbs, and some two-word verbs (like *grow up*) are defined. We like the page numbers written both as numerals and in text (i.e., *two hundred and sixteen*). Unfortunately the typeface is small and blurry-looking so the text is not as readable as it could be. However, comparing price and usefulness this is certainly a 'best buy.'

#9-8

Longman Dictionary of American English, Second Edition (1983, 1997), White Plains, NY: Longman, now Pearson Education. 792pp. ISBN 0-8013-1823-8. A workbook (by Marjorie Fuchs) and a teacher's companion are also available. This dictionary also comes in computer format.

This affordable, portable-sized dictionary is suitable for intermediate through advanced students. With 44,000 words and phrases, most with example sentences as well as definitions, it's a good, medium-weight solution for the preacademic student. Definitions are surprisingly clear—we sometimes refer to this dictionary for help in explaining terms to students. Because of this, even low-intermediate students can use this dictionary.

Each entry has a lot of grammar information, such as irregular verb forms and parts of speech. A nice feature (especially for lower level students) is that verb forms are written out if their spellings vary. Synonyms, opposites and related words are included and in some cases usage notes further explain the contexts in which the word is used. To help students get familiar with using the dictionary, there is a 26-page section on dictionary skills, with exercises for them to try. At the end of the book is a section on word building and a list of irregular verbs. Pronunciation is presented throughout with a modified form of the International Phonetic Alphabet (IPA), which might be very helpful for some students.

For a dictionary that intermediate students can carry around with them, this one teaches them a lot. AS: "This dictionary is my long-standing favorite."

#9-9

The Newbury House Dictionary of American English, Third Edition (1995, 1999) by Philip M. Rideout. Boston: Heinle & Heinle Publishers. 1,032pp. ISBN 0-8384-7812-3. A CD-ROM comes with the book.

This is a 40,000 word learner's dictionary which is still small enough to be portable. Definitions are written in clear, simple language (though not quite as easy as the *Longman,* item #9-8 above) and a sentence is given for each word or use of a word. Modernisms like *carpool* are included and the dictionary is updated annually. The level is suitable for intermediate or high intermediate students.

There are few illustrations, but we like the fairly large print size. The dictionary comes with a pronouncing CD. The introductory passages, explaining how the dictionary is organized, is written in such a way that English learners can read it. One of the best features is the *Activity Guide,* part of the dictionary itself, which provides the learner practice in dictionary skills.

Note: *The Basic Newbury House Dictionary* for beginning students is also available but we haven't yet reviewed it.

#9-10

Random House Webster's Basic Dictionary of American English (1998), New York: Random House; now available from McGraw-Hill. 524pp. ISBN 0-07-228678-4.

This is a very nice learner's dictionary for high intermediate or advanced students. Portable and succinct, with 36,000 words it is similar in size and content to the *Longman*; however, the definitions use a more advanced level of English and are more challenging to understand. There are many examples but they are sometimes given as phrases rather than complete sentences. There is quite a bit of modern vocabulary such as *cyberspace* and *Velcro*. Pronunciation for each word is given in a modified form of IPA. The grammar information is helpful although less extensive than that in the *Longman*. It has few illustrations.

#9-11

Oxford American Wordpower Dictionary (1998), Ruth Urbom, editor. New York: Oxford University Press. 792pp. ISBN 0-19-431319-0. An interactive CD-ROM and a workbook are also available.

This is a very readable dictionary, suitable for high intermediate students in an adult program. The definitions are more complex than those in the *Longman* dictionary above, but they provide two and sometimes three example sentences for many entries, which is very helpful to learners. Unlike other Oxford text dictionaries we've looked at, this one doesn't have an academic slant, so it's suitable for students with many backgrounds and interests.

There are some nice, small illustrations scattered throughout and a 'study pages' section that includes some vocabulary illustrations. One thing we especially like about this book is that idioms and phrasal verbs are defined and clearly marked; this is a feature you won't find in most portable dictionaries. Verb forms are handled in the same way as in the *Longman*; if they have spelling variations they are written out.

#9-12

Collins COBUILD Learner's Dictionary (1996), London: HarperCollins Publishers, available from distributors (see Chapter 13). 1,322pp. ISBN 0-00-375058-2. A workbook is also available.

This is another dictionary intended for intermediate through advanced ESL students. With 60,000 references it is quite a bit more extensive than the books above, yet it is still portable (just barely) and affordable. To compare the definitions in this book to the other dictionaries at this level we would say they are more complex (and more advanced) than the *Longman* above.

The examples for each entry are in complete sentences (not just phrases) and are taken from real usage such as newspapers, magazines, fiction, broadcasts and speech. This makes for very interesting and relevant examples, but with much more involved language than an intermediate student typically deals with. The tone of this dictionary is modern rather than classic—you'll find an entry for *mad cow disease*, for example. A student who is reading mainstream newspapers in English would find this resource very useful.

Full grammar information is included in each entry, and verb forms are always helpfully written out. Pronunciation is given with IPA symbols. The unique feature of this dictionary is the information on word frequency. A typical entry word is marked on a scale of one to five to let you know how often it is actually used in English (this is based on a computer project called the *Bank of English*). This tells the student how important each word is. At the end of the book are lists of words in each frequency category. This is interesting information, and useful also for any teacher who is creating educational materials for ESL.

#9-13

NTC's American English Learner's Dictionary: The Essential Vocabulary of American Language and Culture (1998) by Richard A. Spears, Editor-in-Chief. Chicago: NTC/Contemporary Publishing Group, Inc. 1,090pp. ISBN 0-8442-5860-1.

Unfortunately this dictionary is too large to be easily portable. It is readable, thoughtful and articulate throughout, with definitions that are clear without being oversimplified, and most words have *two* example sentences, which we think is a good feature. The entries, just 22,000 of them, are not meant to be comprehensive but are rather selected as the vocabulary ESL learners most need to acquire. Overall there is a bit less focus on form and grammar in this text than in the other dictionaries at this level; it is intended that students use this resource to focus on meaning.

Like the *Collins* dictionary above, the tone of this work is more modern than classic, but it is less extensive than the *Collins* and less advanced. It is probably most appropriate for intermediate students who still need to do a lot of reading to acquire enough language to move to an advanced level.

Our ideal use of this dictionary would be as a classroom tool—say a class set of them?—to enhance many different kinds of language learning activities.

#9-14

Longman Language Activator: The World's First Production Dictionary (1993), Essex, England: Longman Group UK Ltd., now Pearson Education. 1,587pp. ISBN 0-582-04093-0.

It is hard to describe how unique this book is, and how useful it could be, especially for advanced students learning to express their ideas in writing, but even for ESL teachers in planning interesting lessons. The book is organized by ideas, rather than by the alphabetical listing of words. For example, one entry is the concept *obey*, with seven separate meanings identified. Each meaning is described by several different terms, such as *comply with, take orders from*, etc. Each of these terms is defined and explained with examples. In this case, *obey* has a total of 30 entries. If you were looking for the best words and phrases to describe the concept that children should obey their parents, for example, reading through these entries would give you lots of good ideas and the appropriate terms to use.

We think this is also a useful tool for ESL lesson preparation. What are some of the ways we express the concept of being *sorry*? How many examples of this can you think of? You are sure to find a lot of them here to select from for discussions and vocabulary lessons.

Special Purpose Dictionaries

#9-15

Street Talk 1: How to Speak and Understand American Slang (1992) by David Burke. Los Angeles: Optima Books. 270pp. ISBN 1-879440-00-8. An audio tape cassette is also available; a CD-ROM is forthcoming.

This book and its accompanying cassettes can be used for reference, independent study or class work. It includes common slang such as "chill out!" and "wimp" (including some vulgarisms) with pronunciation, explanation and dialogues. Words and phrases are arranged topically, such as shopping, cars, work and restaurants. It is an advanced book, probably more appropriate for younger adults. *Street Talk 2: Slang Used by Teens, Rappers, Surfers and Popular American TV Shows* (1992) is for an even younger audience and is less appropriate for adults.

#9-16

Dangerous English 2000! An Indispensable Guide for Language Learners and Others, Third Edition (1980, 1998) by Elizabeth Claire. McHenry: Delta Publishing Company. 202pp. ISBN 1-887744-08-8.

For language you don't teach in the classroom (vulgarisms, street language, sexual terms, swearing) but that your students may need to know, here is a complete resource. The book explains just about every 'embarrassing' term you can think of. For sexual matters, for example, it gives diagrams, formal medical terms, common usage and vulgar usage. It also explains euphemisms! The teacher's notes include thoughtful suggestions for approaching this topic appropriately. (Note: This book is graphic and may not be for everyone.)

Vocabulary

#9-17

Basic Vocabulary Builder: Blackline Masters (1991) by Dorothy Gabel Liebowitz. Lincolnwood: NTC/Contemporary. ISBN 0-8442-9017-3.

This book is designed to be used for teaching basic vocabulary in various languages. It consists of a set of photocopiable pictures illustrating vocabulary items arranged thematically (food, furnishings, weather and others). For each set of pictures there is a word list, notes on relevant grammar and patterns and some activities. Additional pictures and teaching suggestions are available in *Practical Vocabulary Builder* by the same author and there are additional vocabulary activities in the *Basic English Vocabulary Builder Activity Book* by Ruth De Jong.

See also:

A Conversation Book (item *#5-10* in the *Speaking* section), which gives detailed illustrations of real-life scenes; these can be used for vocabulary development.

#9-18

English for Everyday Activities: A Picture Process Dictionary (1999) by Lawrence J. Zwier. Syracuse: New Readers Press. 96pp. ISBN 1-56420-222-4. Audio cassette tapes and workbook materials are also available.

This is an illustrated vocabulary book, something like a picture dictionary, except all 61 of the entries are action sequences with captions, in 8 or 10 steps each. For example, making a salad, taking a taxi, repairing a flat tire, using a cash machine, etc. The captions describe the action in each frame (there are no dialogues or conversations). The focus is on verbs to a greater extent than in other vocabulary books.

Each entry is a mini-story and could be used as a starting point to teach grammar or any language skills. The material could also be used in lifeskills instruction—for example, going to the bank. We think the level is approximately intermediate, but you could adapt it for lower level students and use the pictures in many different ways.

#9-19
Lexicarry: An Illustrated Vocabulary Builder for Second Languages, Second Edition (1984, 1989) by Patrick R. Moran. Brattleboro, VT: Pro Lingua Associates. 128pp. ISBN 0-86647-032-8. A set of 25 wall charts is also available.

The photocopiable drawings in this book have no words on them! Students discuss the pictures and create their own vocabulary lesson and reference tool. Word lists are included in the back, as well as plenty of teaching suggestions. We like the simple cartoon drawings of sequences, such as a man getting change to use a pay phone. It's very useful for beginning level students.

#9-20
The ESL Miscellany: A Treasury of Cultural and Linguistic Information, Second Edition, Revised (1981, 1991) Brattleboro, VT: Pro Lingua Associates. 292pp. ISBN 0-86647-043-3.

This is a useful book of vocabulary lists on a wide variety of topics, such as: disasters, recreation, food, history, U.S. culture and grammar, suitable for beginning through intermediate students and photocopiable. It's a good resource for making your own lessons.

See also:
The Card Book (item #4-22 in the *Activities* section) for beginning level activities accompanied by pictures that are helpful for learning and practicing vocabulary.

#9-21
Vocabulary (1986) by John Morgan and Mario Rinvolucri. Oxford: Oxford University Press. 136pp. ISBN 0-19-437091-7.

In this book the authors present over a hundred different techniques for teaching vocabulary. Their aim is to present vocabulary in such a way that the student feels "ownership" of the new words. The activities can be used at all levels. AT: "I always find books by Rinvolucri inspiring. His activities are sophisticated but not difficult to carry out."

Other sources of vocabulary lessons:

Items around you: Anything and everything in your learning space can be used for vocabulary lessons, including the furniture, classroom objects and the people themselves.

Junk mail and catalogs: Many ESL teachers use pictures from clothing catalogs, supermarket flyers, seed catalogs, and other advertisements to create colorful learning materials for their students. With a pile of catalogs as a resource, students can create their own charts and posters as well. These can be the basis for many kinds of language activities.

Pleasure reading: There is no better way to acquire new vocabulary than through regular pleasure reading! See our chapter on *Reading* for ideas on setting up a library of fun reading materials for your students.

Other activities and games: Vocabulary can be learned and reinforced through many of the classroom ideas mentioned in our *Activities* chapter.

Idioms

Most people don't realize how idiomatic the English language really is. Natural speech and text by native speakers is permeated with phrases whose meanings are not literal. These may not be taught in most ESL classes, particularly at the lower levels. To become fluent in English, however, students will have to learn a great many idioms, both actively (knowing how to use them) and passively (knowing what they mean).

We both think that teaching idioms is tricky. Because idioms are so often not literal, and because their meanings change depending on very small prepositions (i.e., *shut up*, *shut off*, *shut out*, etc.), they are hard to remember. In addition, many idioms are appropriate only in certain contexts. The problem with most idioms texts for ESL, in our opinion, is that they introduce too many new idioms at once, making it hard for students to absorb, comprehend or remember them all.

Little by little

The ideal introduction to idioms is in small doses—say, an 'Idiom of the Week' even for lower level students. Then these can be integrated into the context of the students' other work. It is very helpful for a teacher to have a couple of good idiom books on hand in order to choose or adapt some examples and select a new idiom from time to time.

Most of the texts below are intended for intermediate or higher level students. (Few idiom texts are intended for beginners.) For advanced students preparing for academic work or for the TOEFL exam, it is especially important to focus on idioms. For these students, see the University of Michigan Press (item #13-36) or Heinle & Heinle Publishers (item #13-16) in the *Publishers* section for more advanced idiom textbooks not reviewed here.

#9-22
All Clear! Idioms in Context, Book 2, **Second Edition (1985, 1993) by Helen Kalkstein Fragiadakis. Boston: Heinle & Heinle Publishers. 160pp., ISBN 0-8384-3966-7. An audio cassette tape is also available.**

This intermediate level text has 12 lessons, each one introducing fifteen to twenty idioms. The idioms appear first in a dialogue with a story context; for example a man gets 'cold feet' before his wedding and talks with his friends about it. Following this each idiom is explained, with a couple more examples to make the meaning clear. Some exercises help reinforce the material.

We think this is a lot of idioms for one lesson; however, if the students' level of English is advanced enough that they can understand the dialogues easily, they will be recognizing and identifying the idioms rather than learning them as completely new material. They will be able to guess some of the meanings from the context.

In the same series there is a text for high beginners that teaches common phrases and expressions (item *#5-7* in the *Speaking* section) and one for advanced level students with more idioms (not reviewed here).

#9-23

Everyday Idioms for Reference and Practice, Books 1 and 2 (1996) by Ronald E. Feare. White Plains: Addison Wesley Longman, now Pearson Education. Book 1 is 168pp., ISBN 0-201-83408-1. An audio cassette tape is also available for each level.

This book is intended for intermediate or advanced students. There are 50 short units in each book, for a total of over 1200 idioms. Each unit presents six to ten idioms by explaining each one and giving two examples for each. A few exercises for practice follow. There are some line drawings but unfortunately no story that uses the idioms in context. As we explained in the introduction above, this number of new idioms seems like too many for students to learn at once, but because of the clever way the units are organized, the book is nonetheless very useful.

Each unit covers either a day-to-day theme, like getting up in the morning (*wake up, get ready, get going*, etc.) or a functional theme such as participating (*take part in, team up with, be left out*, etc.). The idioms in each unit are ones you would use in the same context, for example idioms about using the telephone. Because the topics are common ones, you can easily select a unit that corresponds to your other ESL materials and find an idiom or idioms appropriate for the level of your students. This book makes an excellent reference tool for teachers' lesson planning and is a useful supplement to other language learning texts.

See also:

Street Talk (item *#9-15* in the *Dictionaries* section above), which references some idioms along with slang.

#9-24

Take it Easy: American Idioms (1981) by Pamela McPartland. Englewood Cliffs: Prentice Hall Regents, now Pearson Education. 210pp. ISBN 0-13-882902-0. An audio cassette tape is also available. (A new edition has since been published, which we have not yet reviewed.)

For high intermediate or advanced students, this book is an in-depth way to get familiar with some of the most important and most-used idioms. Each of the 12 chapters begins with a reading passage on an interesting topic such as how McDonald's Corporation was started, how Levi's jeans were invented, etc. The story includes a dozen or more idioms whose meaning the students try to guess in context. For example, the company 'branched out' quickly and there are now 6,000 restaurants around the world. Following this are many exercises (more than in any other idioms text) to reinforce and practice these using all four skills. One of these chapters would be more than a full sessions' work.

#9-25

VIDIOMS: Activation Idioms for ESL (1991) by John F. Chabot. Virgil, Ontario: Full Blast Productions. A three-video set with reproducible workbook, 209pp. ISBN 1-895451-02-7.

If you're trying to find a way to make idioms memorable, use these videos! Each idiom is presented in three short, humorous skits that make its meaning clear in the context of daily life. In one, for example, a man is grilling outdoors when the phone rings. He asks a friend to "keep an eye on" his hamburger while he goes in to answer the phone. (While he is gone, his friend eats the hamburger.)

Ninety common idioms are demonstrated in this way—all in natural situations that are amusing to watch. Although these are amateur actors, the meanings are very clear and the writing is clever. Students will find the same characters in recurring situations using different idioms. Although the material was designed for intermediate or advanced students, in smaller doses you could use this with lower level students as well. AS: "This would be my preferred way to teach idioms."

CHAPTER 10

English for Specific Purposes

In addition to general all-purpose ESL courses, there are many classes established for a specific purpose. We've included here materials on survival skills, workplace, and citizenship education. (We have not included workplace materials for specific professions, such as airline pilots or bankers, nor for business or academic purposes as these fall outside the focus of this book.)

For new arrivals

A *survival* course (or component) is especially intended to give students the basic information they need to survive in their new environment, immediately upon their arrival. This kind of instruction is sometimes called 'lifeskills training,' 'coping skills' or 'survival skills.'

Working language

Increasingly there are courses designed specifically to teach English to people working in a particular factory, restaurant or hotel or to those who are preparing to begin work. Such *workplace* classes often include language and information (calling in sick, using time clocks, measuring and mixing cleaning chemicals) specific to a given workplace. These courses can also include general language instruction.

Many ESL programs now have *work readiness* components, due to current funding and new mandates. Lessons geared toward work readiness focus on more general skills typically needed in any workplace and are not oriented toward certain types of work or careers. For these courses, the 'SCANS' guidelines can help teachers and programs know what kinds of skills are important (see glossary entry for more information on SCANS).

Becoming citizens

Another type of class for a specific purpose is established to prepare students for *citizenship* tests. Along with books on citizenship, we have included the website of the Immigration and Naturalization Service (INS). Immigration law changes frequently and the website provides up-to-date information that might affect the test. Finally, citizenship can mean a lot more than just passing the test, so we include a few resources on *civic participation*.

Survival Skills

The students who need this kind of basic information, like how to get a driver's license, what to say to the landlord, how to open a bank account, what to do in an emergency, etc., are usually brand-new arrivals. If their English skills are very limited, it can be vitally important that they learn some of this information right away, like how to call 9-1-1, for example. Some of this instruction depends on the needs of the students and on your specific location. Many teachers (or their programs) design customized materials, sometimes in consultation with former students who can remember what they needed to know when they first arrived.

A few titles offer a starting point for survival skills instruction. Such skills are also integrated into many coursebooks (see Chapter 2).

#10-1
Lifelines: Coping Skills in English, **Books 1–4, Second Edition (1981, 1993) by Barbara Foley and Howard Pomann. Upper Saddle River: Prentice Hall Regents, now Pearson Education. Book 1 is 128pp, ISBN 0-13-529538-6.**

This book takes a 'competency-based' approach to lifeskills, which means it tries to teach students how to deal with certain situations—for example, how to return an item to a store, how to introduce yourself, how to call the landlord and how to take a phone message. Each chapter begins with a model dialogue (for example, a tenant calling her landlord to report a leaking pipe), which students can listen to and practice. Students look at several pictures of other apartment problems and practice the same dialogue with different examples, such as an outlet that isn't working. Students are given vocabulary cues so they can practice these situations. A *Concentration*-style game is provided to reinforce the lesson as well as some short written exercises. A follow-up picture, for example a drawing of a building with six apartments in which water is leaking everywhere, gives students more practice talking about the vocabulary and can be used for writing as well.

While this book also presents a lot of new vocabulary in a very structured way, the material has the advantage over *Speaking of Survival* (#10-3 below) in that the contexts are a bit more interesting and fun. The levels range from beginning through intermediate, but literacy skills are required to use this material. It might be used as a supplement to a regular program.

#10-2

Survival English: English Through Conversations, Books 1, 2 and 3, Second Edition (1985, 1994) by Lee Mosteller and Michele Haight. Englewood Cliffs: Prentice Hall Regents, now Pearson Education. Book 1 is 260pp. ISBN 0-13-016635-9. A teacher's manual with reproducible activities is available for each level.

This series is written at a very beginning level, and though not intended for students with no literacy skills at all, it is suitable for low beginners, even those with little education. It provides students with information and practice about many kinds of everyday needs, including filling out forms, reading labels, comparing prices, paying bills, reading schedules, writing a note to the landlord. These topics are nicely presented with short dialogues, which the students can practice. Simple exercises help to reinforce the material. For example, we like the one in which students have to interpret medication instructions such as "2 tsp. every 4 hrs.," by writing out 'teaspoons' or 'tablespoons' to indicate how much. All of the exercises are relevant to specific needs the students may have; the material is clear, uncluttered and not intimidating. It is not intended to provide a complete language course, however, and should be seen as supplementary material.

#10-3

Speaking of Survival (1982), Daniel B. Freeman. New York: Oxford University Press. 228pp. ISBN 0-19-503110-5. An audio cassette tape is also available.

Although this is not as flashy as many more recent books, it does a good job of covering the basics of "what people say" in a variety of real-life conversations, with an emphasis on vocabulary. Topics include banking, shopping, school, hospital, etc. Each chapter presents a picture with about 25 labeled items. For example, in the first chapter we see a doctor checking a patient, with stethoscope, tongue depressor, mouth, etc. indicated. Some additional pictures show more items in detail—thermometer, pill, etc. Following the vocabulary section are two picture stories about going to the doctor, presented as dialogues. Students can listen and read the conversations. Next comes sentence pattern practice, in which students practice phrases often used in this context ("My stomach hurts," etc.) Several short written activities are included and students are asked to roleplay the conversations. Two short reading passages, for example about getting an annual check-up and what to do if you are sick, are included with follow-up questions. A final section asks students to gather local information, for example using the phone book. The book is appropriate for intermediate level students, or high beginners if they already have literacy skills. The book and accompanying tape are reasonably priced.

See also:

English for Everyday Activities (item #9-18 in the *Vocabulary* section); the picture series in this material can be adapted for teaching lifeskills topics.

LifePrints (item #2-4 in the *Coursebooks* section) for many detailed lessons on lifeskills topics such as applying for a driver's license. For shorter lessons on the same kinds of topics, see the *Real-Life English* series (item #2-5 in *Coursebooks*).

Workplace and Work Readiness

Teachers planning a course for a workplace environment need to ascertain the purpose of the course as viewed by the various stake-holders (students, management, the teacher's employers) before deciding on a curriculum. It is helpful to visit the workplace and find out what jobs the students have and what is expected of them. The workplace itself is also a good source of teaching materials (signs, notices, health and safety materials).

For more information on how a workplace program can be organized, see materials published by NCLE (item #13-24 in the *Publishers* section).

#10-4
Day by Day: English for Employment Communication (1994) by Steven J. Molinsky and Bill Bliss. Englewood Cliffs: Prentice Hall Regents, now Pearson Education. 122pp. ISBN 0-13-328238-4. An audio cassette tape is also available.

If you are familiar with *Side by Side* by the same authors, you'll recognize the format in this book. Students are given a model dialogue; several other example situations are presented with small pictures and students have to create new dialogues based on these. The conversations are a bit stilted, but they do contain useful phrases. Although there is a lot of grammar and substitution drill here, the book also contains a great deal of useful workplace vocabulary. Most of the lessons are organized by function (making requests, apologizing, asking permission, etc.) with examples from different work environments. The book also includes readings about a variety of work settings. The introduction says it is for beginners; it would be better for high beginning or intermediate students in adult programs.

#10-5
English ASAP™: Connecting English to the Workplace, Literacy level and Books 1–4 (1999). Austin: Steck-Vaughn. Book 1 is 133pp, ISBN 0-8172-7951-2. Workbooks, audio cassette tapes and teacher's editions are also available for each level. (See item #3-10 in the *Literacy* section for a more detailed review of the literacy level book.)

This is a five-level series with student books, teacher's editions, cassettes and workbooks based on realistic workplace language and situations. Each chapter covers a different topic, for example: communication, technology, time management, customer service, finances, health and safety. Because each level covers the same topics, different levels could be used in a multilevel class, with all students studying the same topic. One thing we like about this series is that the topics are general enough to apply to many different kinds of workplaces, for example safety equipment and safety rules for various kinds of jobs are discussed; students practice reading some safety instructions and filling out an accident report. They also learn what to do when they see an unsafe situation. The material incorporates SCANS concepts that teach students strategies they need in the workplace. The student books also include tips on culture and language learning.

The series integrates all four language skills and grammar, but lacks extended readings; if supplemented with some readings this series could provide a core text for beginning and intermediate students.

#10-6

ESL for Action: Problem Posing at Work (1987) by Elsa Roberts Auerbach and Nina Wallerstein. Reading: Addison Wesley Publishing Company, now Pearson Education. 176pp. ISBN 0-201-00101-2. A teacher's guide is also available.

This is one of the few workplace textbooks which is suitable for a wide range of work settings because it focuses on human issues rather than specific on-the-job vocabulary. It suggests ways to raise and resolve problems in the workplace: how to ask about job benefits, whether or not to work overtime, making sure the workers understand what is said to them, clarifying information about benefits and understanding the rights of a worker. Many readings about real-life dilemmas provide interesting examples for discussion. Several exercises in each unit provide opportunities for the students to reflect on their own experiences; for this reason the book is probably most effective for students who are already working. The complex and important issues in this book are presented in a thoughtful way. The book is appropriate for intermediate and advanced students but some of it could be adapted for high beginners.

We recommend the teacher's guide for anyone who wishes to better understand the problem-posing approach and incorporate it into their regular teaching.

#10-7

Let's Work Safely: English Language Skills for Safety in the Workplace (1984) by Linda Mrowicki. Palatine: Linmore Publishing. 114pp. ISBN 0-916591-00-X. A teacher's book is also available.

This is an excellent lower level text focusing on workplace safety. It is well-illustrated and provides the student with plenty of communicative activities, including roleplays. It deals with basic issues such as injuries, accidents and appropriate clothing and behavior in the workplace. Working students can contribute a lot from their own experience. There is a teacher's manual for the book.

#10-8

May I Help You? Learning How to Interact with the Public (1987) by Heide Spruck Wrigley. Reading: Addison Wesley Publishing Company, now Pearson Education. 153pp. ISBN 0-201-09943-8. A teacher's guide and an audio cassette tape are also available; the tape is an important part of the material. (This book has now gone out of print but may be found in libraries and resource centers.)

This vocational book is intended for intermediate learners who deal with the public in their jobs. It is arranged by functions (i.e., understanding what the customer wants, dealing with complaints) and contains useful language and situational practice. For example, in the chapter on dealing with complaints, students look at a photo and listen to an incident on tape in which a customer complains about her hamburger. Then students give their opinions about how the incident was handled. A second taped scenario provides a different example, which the students discuss, then they compare the two events. Next, students take turns roleplaying the customer in the restaurant scene, while the other students mark down their observations on a checklist (Was the waitress trying to be helpful? etc.). The next section gives detailed examples of five ways to handle a complaint. Another exercise asks students to list what is reasonable and unreasonable in various situations. More activities include detailed roleplays for practice, reading and writing (such as a letter of complaint) and making observations in the real world.

We like the way the students' observations and judgment are built into the material in this book. There is a nice blend here of language study and social skills practice.

#10-9

People at Work: Listening and Communicative Skills Vocabulary Building (1990) by Edgar Sathow, Catherine Sadow and George Draper. Brattleboro, VT: Pro Lingua. 106pp. ISBN 0-86647-037-9. Audio cassette tapes and a teacher's book are also available.

This listening book is intended for intermediate or advanced students and can be used as part of a class or independently. In most adult classes it would be suitable for advanced students. Each of the 10 lessons consists of a fairly long recorded interview with a real person about their job. Students are encouraged to guess the meaning of new vocabulary in context. The interview is followed by additional activities, including projects for students to undertake outside of class. It is a very interesting and creative book.

#10-10

Workskills Books 1, 2 and 3 (1996) by Mary Lou Byrne, Susan C. Quatrini and Kathy S. Van Ormer. Upper Saddle River: Prentice Hall Regents, now Pearson Education. Book 1 is 128pp, ISBN 0-13-953076-2. A teacher's guide and audio cassette tapes are also available.

This series is organized according to concepts that are important for all work environments; for example, interacting with supervisors, resolving conflicts, using teamwork, and goal setting. Students approach these topics through anecdotes that they read or listen to, then they are encouraged to analyze and propose solutions to these cases. We like the integration of math and graphing skills into every chapter along with the other four-skill language practice. There are some nice, realistic problem-solving tasks using math skills and listening, and good interactive activities.

Each level approaches the same topics in a different way, so the series can be used with a multilevel class. The levels range from high beginning through intermediate, but the vocabulary will seem more challenging than other books at these levels. The content of this series has quite a bit of depth to it and reflects the true complexity and challenge of an adult's working life.

#10-11

The Working Culture: Cross-Cultural Communication for New Americans, Books 1 and 2 (1989) by David Hemphill, Barbara Pfaffenberger and Barbara Hockman. Englewood Cliffs: Prentice Hall Regents, now Pearson Education. Book 1 is 110pp., ISBN 0-13-965187-X.

Much of the material in this book could be used in a culture or discussion class separate from the workplace, as the issues considered are applicable to all newcomers. The authors see it as a book for enhancing communication and not as one for teaching language itself. It is an excellent resource for teachers who want their intermediate and advanced students to consider cultural issues.

See also:

The Working Experience (item #6-15 in the *Reading* section), which includes short, easy-to-read stories by students about their experiences with work.

#10-12

Working It Out: Interactive English for the Workplace (1998) by Ronna Magy. Boston: Heinle & Heinle Publishers. 144pp. ISBN: 0-8384-8135-3. An audio cassette tape is also available.

Every chapter in this book has two 'Work Stories' written by immigrants about their job experiences. Each story is accompanied by a nice color photo, and the stories are long enough and complex enough that we get a good understanding of each person's life. Some follow-up activities give students a chance to discuss the story and talk about their own experiences.

This textbook would be excellent for an intermediate class which prepares students to enter the workplace. Much of it focuses on getting and beginning a new job. It includes a variety of material—not only the readings but also listening exercises, charts, photographs and discussion of problem solving in the workplace. Students learn in detail about such topics as pay checks, benefits and safety at work.

We think this book would be a good choice for students whose language level is too advanced for *English ASAP* (item #10-5)—high beginners or intermediates. It covers many of the same issues in more detail. AS: "I think students will be very interested in the stories."

Citizenship Test Preparation

In the past few years, passing the citizenship test has become an urgent necessity for many of our students. Benefits which used to be available to foreign residents are increasingly available only to citizens. Because of this, more students than ever are eager for instruction that will help them study for this test. The following list includes titles that present the information typically found on the citizenship exam.

Most of these books are slender volumes. They provide basic information, usually in as brief a form as possible. Because of this, the information is dense and often abstract. This makes it very hard for beginning level students or students who are new to this country to understand. It will be up to the teacher to expand on these lessons to make them comprehensible—by telling stories, bringing in photos, showing videos, taking field trips, inviting guest speakers—whatever will make the subject real for the students. It will also be up to the teacher to know if the testing process has changed since the citizenship materials were printed.

One warning to teachers—remember that unless you are also an attorney you must not give legal advice to students. In case you are wrong, that bad advice is far worse than no advice at all. If students have a question about their status or other immigration issues, you should refer them to an immigration lawyer or to an agency that can provide legal services.

#10-13
By the People, For the People: U.S. Government and Citizenship (1992, 1995) by **Deborah J. Short, Margaret Seufert-Bosco, Allene Guss Grognet. McHenry, IL: Delta Systems Co./CAL. 173pp. ISBN 0-937354-69-4.**

For high intermediate or advanced students with good literacy skills, this is an interesting and detailed text. Each of the 32 chapters includes pre-reading discussion questions, a vocabulary exercise or puzzle, and a reading of 3 or 4 paragraphs. The topics include *The Thirteen Colonies, The Articles of Confederation,* and *The First President.* Some quiz questions follow each reading. In addition, information about each topic is presented in chart or graph form. The students use this information to answer the questions.

We find the charts and drawings throughout to be helpful. For example, a chart explaining the Constitution diagrams what each article is about (instead of just reprinting the original document as in some textbooks). A chart about local government and what services it provides is especially interesting, and probably useful for the students. (*Of the People: U.S. History* by the same authors is similar, but we found it less useful. It condenses so much information in a short space that it seems hard to comprehend.)

#10-14

Citizenship Made Simple: An Easy to Read Guide to the U.S. Citizenship Process (1996) by Barbara Brooks Kimmel and Alan M. Lubiner. Chester, NJ: Next Decade, Inc.; available from Delta Systems Co. 78pp. ISBN 0-9626003-3-4.

This is an excellent reference work on the process of applying for citizenship as well as on the content the applicant must know. The information is written by an immigration consultant and an immigration lawyer. They give the requirements for applying, a list of the 100 sample questions and answers, some sample forms and addresses of INS offices in the U.S. This book is not for beginning students—no attempt is made to provide teaching activities, and little explanation is given. The best use for this material might be as a teacher reference or as information for advanced students. (Note: The most up-to-date source for this kind of information is from the INS itself. See their website listed below, item #10-20.)

#10-15

Citizenship Now: A Guide for Naturalization (1990) by Aliza Becker and Laurie Edwards in cooperation with Travelers and Immigrants Aid of Chicago. Chicago: NTC/Contemporary Books. 165pp. ISBN 0-8092-3270-7. An audio cassette tape is also available.

This is intended as a textbook for a citizenship class. It provides short readings with information about U.S. history and government with good comprehension and vocabulary exercises. Timelines and charts help to make the information easier to understand. Like many citizenship texts, the book provides plenty of practice dictations (these are included on the cassette, so students could practice them on their own). There are also some exercises to practice English structures relevant to the test, such as tag questions.

There is quite a bit of in-depth information here that would be of interest even to students not preparing for the test. For example, the book includes a description of the two major political parties and their differences and a discussion of the Miranda decision. Some of this is difficult material and is not written for beginners. There are sample forms for the students to practice on, and the list of 100 questions with the answer printed below each one. Although this is not the most recent material available, it is a solid and useful text for intermediate students and up.

#10-16

Citizenship: Passing the Test (1998) by Lynne Weintraub. Syracuse: New Readers Press. 191pp. ISBN 1-56420-205-4. An audio cassette tape is also available.

This is the only citizenship text really and truly written for students at a beginning reading level. It does have readings, in the form of 3 or 4 short sentences on each topic, but these are presented with large pictures to help make the meaning clear. Follow-up exercises include matching pictures to words and words to phrases, true or false questions and some fill-in-the-blanks. The book places emphasis on copying sentences for practice and using these to practice dictations. Multiple-choice quizzes help accustom students to this form of test-taking.

Throughout, the drawings are surprisingly good at conveying meaning. For example, how do you explain the Bill of Rights and freedom of assembly at this level? A simple drawing of average citizens attending a public meeting tells the story perfectly. This text is indispensable for low-level citizenship students.

#10-17

English Through Citizenship (1989) by Elaine Kirn. McHenry: Delta Systems Co. Student Book Intermediate A is 92pp, ISBN 0-937354-41-4. Literacy level, Beginning and Intermediate B are also available.

There are four books in this series of textbooks for citizenship classes: literacy, beginning, and intermediate A and B. Although the series isn't new, it provides some very nice exercises you won't find in other books. For example, there are exercises about interpreting the sample forms (in Intermediate Level A)—most texts just reprint these forms. There are maps the students have to write on, instead of just look at, and a *Battleship*-type letter game to practice listening and writing letters and numbers. In the Beginning Level text, much of the information is presented in picture series. For example, the history of immigration in the U.S. is presented with 20 small pictures that enhance the written text and timeline. (The Literacy Level text is not as useful; for these students you'd be better off with *Citizenship: Passing the Test*, item #10-16 above.) Two short units at the end are specifically on California and Los Angeles. There is a teacher's guide for each level.

#10-18

English Through Citizenship: A Question-and-Answer Game (1989) by Elaine Kirn. Etcetera Graphics; available through Alta Book Center Publishers. ISBN 60-0095-0017.

This board game with citizenship quiz cards might be a fun way for students to review the material they are studying. The questions are in six categories (*U.S. History*; *the Constitution*; *Geography*; *Federal Government*; *State and Local Government*; *Symbols, Holidays* and *People*). The questions are based on INS textbooks, so they cover what the students need to know. We thought the questions were pretty difficult, so this game might be most appropriate for students who have already studied quite a bit of citizenship material.

#10-19

The INS Citizenship Interview: Will They Pass? A 52-minute video (1996) published by Powerhouse Publishing in Los Angeles; distributed by New Readers Press (see #13-26 in the *Publishers* section).

This video has three parts, all of which might be useful in helping your students prepare for their citizenship interview. First, we see a complete interview, in which a young man applying for citizenship is asked nearly fifty questions about his application, is given 10 questions to read and answer about the U.S. government, and is asked to write a dictation sentence. The man is well-prepared, asks for clarification a couple of times but clearly passes. Second, the INS criteria for passing are listed one by one, and we see several students responding to individual questions. This gives your students plenty of time to consider these requirements. Finally, we see some clips and are asked to evaluate whether each student will pass. This last part is interesting, but we think it's most suited for students who are already pretty well prepared for the exam, as some of the issues are complicated. The tape may be useful both for study and for encouragement.

#10-20
INS website, http://www.ins.usdoj.gov

This government website for the U.S. Immigration and Naturalization Service provides current information on applying for citizenship. Sample test questions are given and forms can be downloaded or ordered online. Select 'FAQs' (Frequently Asked Questions) from the top of the main page for clear answers on specific questions about the application process.

#10-21
LifePrints: ESL for Adults, **Book 2 (1993) by Christy M. Newman. Syracuse: New Readers Press. 128pp, ISBN 0-88336-035-7.**

See Chapter 10 in Book 2 of this series for a unit about becoming a citizen, written for high beginning students. There are several clever activities here, including an interview activity called 'Who's ready?' in which students ask each other questions to find out who meets the minimum requirements for applying for citizenship. The Teacher's Resource File (TRF) for this unit has a nice activity about different categories of freedom. Students read an example and decide if it falls under freedom of speech, assembly or press. This is a very good way to get beginning level students talking about advanced concepts. (For more about this textbook series, see item #2-4 in the *Coursebook* section.)

#10-22
U.S. Citizen, Yes: Interactive Citizenship Preparation **(1996) by Ronna Magy. Boston: Heinle & Heinle Publishers. 102pp. ISBN 0-8384-6714-8. An audio cassette tape is also available.**

This is one of the few citizenship texts that tries to provide interactive activities in addition to the usual readings, timelines and comprehension questions. The end of each chapter also has review questions in the form of a board game. The book could be used with beginning or intermediate students. There is a 10-page section in the back that provides a series of pictures to introduce the material in each chapter to beginning students. This makes it possible to use the book with a multilevel class. Finally, the 100 typical questions in the back are presented in the best possible format—with the answers in a column on the right. Students can easily cover the answers with a sheet of paper and practice on their own.

#10-23

Voices of Freedom: English and Civics for the U.S. Citizenship Exam, Second Edition (1989, 1994) by Bill Bliss with Steven J. Molinsky. Englewood Cliffs: Prentice Hall Regents, now Pearson Education. 178pp. ISBN 0-13-035684-0. A teacher's guide and audio cassette tapes are also available.

For high beginning or low intermediate students who are literate, this is a fairly clear and simple text with information about history and government that does not seem overwhelming. We like the sample interviews throughout each chapter, which the students practice in the role of INS examiner and applicant. This also gives some basic instruction in filling out forms. There are numerous practice quizzes and dictations to get students accustomed to test-taking. Photographs sprinkled throughout enhance the text. The 100 questions and answers are presented in two columns so students can easily test themselves. All in all, this book may be a 'best buy.'

#10-24

The Way to U.S. Citizenship, New Edition (1989, 1997) by Margaret W. Hirschy and Patricia L. Hirschy. Carlsbad: Dominie Press, Inc. 160pp. ISBN 1-56270-972-0.

This intermediate text has longer readings than some other citizenship books—most are a full page or longer. The material is well-written and conveys a lot of information without seeming as 'dense' as the readings in other textbooks. Comprehension exercises follow each of the 36 lessons. There are maps and some charts, but no pictures. The book has a Spanish glossary, making it especially useful for Spanish-speaking students. The 100 typical questions are followed by an answer key on separate pages.

Civic Participation

For those students not preparing for the test, or who have already passed, learning how government works in practice is still very important, especially if they wish to take an active role in the community. Here are some starting points for this kind of information.

#10-25

Citizen Handbook, A Practical Guide to Everyday Citizenship (1993) by James E. Davis and Sharryl Davis. Jointly published by: National Council for the Social Studies, Instructional Design Associates and Educational Extension Systems; available from EES (P.O. Box 472, Waynesboro, PA 17268, 1-800-447-8561). 92pp. ISBN 0-87986-062-6.

This inexpensive handbook is not intended for test preparation, but is about the rights and responsibilities of every citizen. It includes information about the usual citizenship topics such as registering to vote, paying taxes and serving on juries, as well as about job hunting, insurance, managing money, the court system and the structure of the U.S. government from federal down to local. For each topic, there is a page for students to note down information that pertains especially to them or to the state or local community where they live. The reading level is fairly high, but each section is brief. The book includes plenty of topics for class discussion (whom do you call to report a pothole?) and it is a useful resource that students will annotate, keep and refer to in the future.

#10-26
The League of Women Voters website, http://www.lwv.org/

The League of Women Voters was started originally to educate women about political processes and issues when women first got the vote in 1920. Today they are still educating voters, regardless of gender. Their publications are extremely useful, especially before a national election. Since these materials are often updated, we've given you their website address so that you can search for what is currently available. Their website also includes nonpartisan information on government, campaign finance reform, health and environmental concerns and social policy. In many cases, this material will be too advanced for your students, but it might at least give you the information you need to explain issues to your students in class.

Culture and Community Life

Language is just one part of our culture—the history, customs, holidays and other aspects of community life are important for students to learn as well. These cultural matters often form an integral part of an ESL class. Learning about culture can help students get oriented, understand what's going on around them, and even make them feel a part of things in their new country.

In this section we've collected materials that cover culture (specifically North American culture). Some of these are student texts, and some you might be more likely to use as a teacher reference to help you integrate cultural material into your lessons.

This section includes: *Culture and History*, *Holidays*, and *Community Resources*.

Culture and History

#11-1

America's Story, Books 1 and 2 (1995) by Vivian Bernstein. Austin: Steck-Vaughn Co. Book 1 is 140pp, ISBN 0-8114-2791-9. A teacher's guide and a teacher's resource binder are also available. (There is also a Spanish language edition of this series.)

These two slim volumes present a remarkable amount of American history in a detailed, clear and balanced way. The contributions of minorities are given recognition throughout. Did you know the Revolutionary war was funded in part by a Jewish American from Poland? That a free African American helped to design the nation's capital? That the Cherokees published their own newspaper in the 1820's? The author succeeds at presenting complicated conflicts, such as the Civil Rights movement, in a straightforward way.

The series is written at a level that intermediate students can read, although they may need help with some vocabulary. Lower level students can enjoy the material too, as the color illustrations are expressive and educational in themselves. Good maps are included in almost every short chapter, as well as a chart of facts with an exercise to help students build graph-reading skills. Short exercises to review the content are also included. The prices are reasonable; this is a 'best buy.'

#11-2

American Voices: Movers and Shakers (1998) by **Julia Jolly. Carlsbad, CA: Dominie Press Inc. 120pp. ISBN 0-7685-0007-9. An audio cassette tape and a teacher's manual are also available.**

This book contains twelve biographies of famous contemporary Americans such as Ruth Bader Ginsburg, Colin Powell and Bill Cosby—people from varied ethnic backgrounds who have succeeded. Success is the main theme of the book, as we learn of the thoughts, fears, struggles and strategies of each individual. Seven or more thoughtful exercises are included in each chapter. These require the students to listen to or read the text carefully to identify concepts, supporting details, etc. Some exercises also encourage discussion about the student's own success strategies.

Although labeled 'low intermediate,' we think this text is challenging even for an intermediate level student in an adult program. The stories are lengthy (8 or 9 paragraphs) and the vocabulary fairly sophisticated. Still, the topics are motivating enough that students will want to read the material, and you could adapt or retell the stories for lower level students.

#11-3

Beyond Language: Cross-cultural Communication, **Second Edition (1982, 1993) by Deena R. Levine & Mara B. Adelman. Englewood Cliffs: Prentice Hall Regents, now Pearson Education. 288pp. ISBN 0-13-094855-1.**

This advanced level cultural reader covers ten aspects of American culture in detail, such as personal relationships, family values, work values, etc. A lengthy reading of nine or ten paragraphs covers various aspects of the topic, for example (in personal relationships), the difference between friendliness and friendship. Comprehension questions and several vocabulary and 'word forms' exercises follow. Discussion topics give students a chance to talk about their own experiences and culture; for example about their own friends, how they met and what activities they share. Finally, students are given a case study (or other reading) to read and discuss in groups. Additional questions are offered for cross-cultural discussion.

This text is for students who are really interested in why Americans do what they do. If the level of reading is too high for your students, you may find it an excellent resource for your own information, to help explain cultural matters to your students or to get ideas for class discussion. In the family values chapter, for example, the questionnaire on who does what in the household would be interesting for students at any level.

See also:
Culturally Speaking (item #5-11 in the *Speaking* section), which provides students with practice speaking in a variety of social situations and offers the opportunity for some cross-cultural comparisons.

#11-4

English at Home and on the Road (1991, 1996) by Michael Sudlow. Monmouth, OR: Excellence in Education Publications. 130pp. ISBN 1-877591-00-9. A teacher's manual is also available.

Don't be fooled by the modest appearance of this book—it's more useful than it looks. Each of the 12 units has a reading on an aspect of American life such as food, shopping, driving and holiday customs. The reading is prefaced by a page of vocabulary organized by category for the students to discuss or add to (for example food is divided into drinks, desserts, etc.). Several grammar exercises give students practice using this vocabulary, such as using comparatives to talk about which food is more delicious. A page of idiom practice is included (i.e., "I'm in the mood for pizza"). Students read a dialogue and do a roleplay. A reading activity with a newspaper ad or other graphic asks students to figure something out (if it's $1.89 on sale and you save $.67, what is the regular price?)

Our favorite part of each chapter is the clever speaking activity. In the food chapter, it's a supermarket maze that the students play like a board game, buying each item they land on. The student with the lowest bill at the end wins. Some writing and review activities follow this. The book has a light touch of humor and would be pleasant to teach from.

This book is appropriate for low-intermediate or intermediate students who already have basic survival and literacy skills but need to expand their vocabularies and practice speaking and listening. A companion text, *Listening to English at Home and on the Road* with an accompanying audio cassette tape provides structured listening exercises on the same topics.

#11-5

Face to Face: Communication, Culture and Collaboration, Second Edition (1985, 1993) by Virginia Vogel Zanger. Heinle & Heinle Publishers. 222pp. ISBN 0-8384-3954-3. An instructor's guide is also available.

This book explores cultural topics such as politeness, eating habits, family roles, etc. by first presenting a story with a case study about a misunderstanding. The students read and discuss the story, then read a background passage about American customs. Next, students interview each other with an in-class questionnaire to explore cross-cultural differences. Finally, students are given a similar questionnaire about customs and expectations and are asked to interview an

American (they would do this part out of class). Students then compare and discuss the answers they got in their survey.

High intermediate or advanced students can benefit a lot from this book. It gives them a structured, meaningful way to interact with Americans and teaches cultural expectations through the process of discovery rather than just explaining.

#11-6

Introducing the USA: A Cultural Reader (1993) by Milada Broukal and Peter Murphy. New York: Longman, now Pearson Education. 92pp. ISBN 0-8013-0984-0.

This beginning-level reader provides short reading passages on fun cultural topics such as the origin of peanut butter and the invention of basketball. There are short biographies of famous historical figures such as Harriet Tubman and Thomas Edison. Some useful vocabulary activities are included with each reading. The topics tend to be more amusing than thoughtful, but we think students will appreciate them.

This book is part of a series: *A First Look at the USA* is slightly lower in level, *All About the USA* is low-intermediate and *More About the USA* is intermediate.

See also:

Speaking Naturally (item #5-17 in the *Speaking* section), which gives practice using appropriate language in different social situations.

Talk about Trivia (item #4-34 in the *Activities* section) for a fun way to discuss U.S. culture and history topics.

#11-7

Talking about the U.S.A.: An Active Introduction to American Culture (1996) by Janet Giannotti and Suzanne Mele Szwarcewicz. Upper Saddle River: Prentice Hall Regents, now Pearson Education. 237pp. ISBN 0-295-15962-1. An instructor's manual (including tapescripts) and an audio cassette tape are also available.

While most books on culture aim to present cultural content through readings, this text seeks to provide lots of listening, speaking and grammar exercises in the context of culture and history. For example, in a chapter on inventors in American history, students listen to a lecture about five inventors and note down their dates and inventions on a chart. Several follow-up exercises help students learn the new vocabulary. Then in pairs students practice past tense questions ("What did Edison invent?") using the worksheet provided. A relative clause exercise follows ("The light bulb is an invention that . . .") and one on changing active voice to passive ("The lightbulb was invented by . . ."). Students get a chance to discuss other inventions they are familiar with, and a cloze exercise reviews the material. The intended audience is low intermediate students but we think some of the material may be too challenging for that level. It is appropriate for students with a fair amount of previous education.

#11-8

The U.S.A.: Customs and Institutions: A Survey of American Culture and Traditions: An Advanced Reader for ESL and EFL Students (1990) by Ethel Tiersky and Martin Tiersky. Englewood Cliffs: Prentice Hall Regents, now Pearson Education. 304pp. ISBN 0-13-946385-2. A teacher's guide is also available. (A new edition has since been published, which we have not yet reviewed.)

This is a very densely written book for advanced readers covering most aspects of American culture. It is divided into units (such as *American Holidays: Their Origins and Customs*) that range in length from two to nine chapters each. The book has the advantage of putting "everything you want to know" in one book but is of necessity somewhat superficial. The exercises focus more on vocabulary than on comprehension. It would also be a useful resource for teachers who need additional information about the United States.

Holidays

#11-9

American Holidays: Exploring Traditions, Customs and Backgrounds (1986) by Barbara Klebanow and Sara Fischer. Brattleboro: Pro Lingua Associates. 117pp. ISBN 0-86647-018-2.

This book is called a "vocabureader." It describes 16 holidays or events that are celebrated in the U.S. Each holiday is covered in two or three pages, followed by vocabulary and content exercises. The descriptions give historical background as well as information about how the holidays are celebrated. The readings are suitable for high-beginning or intermediate students. AT: "My boss says that teachers are always walking off with this book."

#11-10

Celebrate with Us: A Beginning Reader of Holidays and Festivals (1995, 1997) by James H. Kennedy. Lincolnwood: NTC/Contemporary Books. 190pp. ISBN 0-8092-3413-0.

In addition to the usual American festivals and holidays, this book includes Kwansaa, Chinese New Year, the Cherry Blossom Festival and Cinco de Mayo. The readings are short (one half to three quarters of a page) and are written for beginners. Each unit includes comprehension and vocabulary exercises. AT: "My high-beginning students have enjoyed working with this book. It answers a lot of questions they have about holidays in an easy-to-read format."

#11-11

ESL Teacher's Holiday Activities Kit (1990) by Elizabeth Claire. New York: The Center for Applied Research in Education; available from Prentice Hall Regents (now Pearson Education) and book distributors. 211pp. ISBN 0-87628-305-9.

We've always ignored this book because it is written for a K-12 audience. So many teachers of adult ESL have told us they use it, though, we finally took a look and, sure enough, there are plenty of activities here you can adapt to adult students, especially at the beginning and high-beginning levels. The stories and cultural information about the events might be interesting to anyone not familiar with them. You could use these stories for reading and discussion, and create your own language activities with them.

We like the simple picture stories, for example the story of Thanksgiving, told at the beginning level. Other stories are written at a high-beginning level, but there are small line drawings throughout that help to clarify meanings. There is more here than the usual holidays (Christmas, Hanukkah, etc.) including events like Election Day, Arbor Day, United Nations Day, Fire Prevention Week and even the four seasons. There are some vocabulary exercises provided, and you can select from a list of ideas for further classroom activities.

#11-12
The International Holiday & Festival Primer, Books 1 and 2 (1996) by David De-Rocco, Joan Dundas and Ian Zimmerman. Virgil, Ontario: Full Blast Productions. Book 1 is 150pp, spiral-bound, ISBN 1-895451-24-8.

Each book covers 25 events, including religious holidays, cultural festivals, national holidays, etc. Many of these are events you won't find described in other books on holidays. They cover a wide range of cultures and interests such as *International Women's Day, Diwali* (Hindu), *Earth Day, Zulu Festival* (South Africa), *Carnival* (Brazil) and *Chinese New Year.*

Each story is about 10 paragraphs in length, presented in news column format which is easy to read. The vocabulary might be challenging for intermediate students; the readings are most appropriate for a high intermediate or advanced level. Six comprehension exercises follow each reading, including a crossword puzzle about the story. The stories would provide interesting discussion material for a conversation class of students from various cultures.

The price of the texts might seem high, but they are reproducible, which is a very useful feature.

Community Resources

If it makes sense for students to learn something about the community around them, the best teaching material for doing so should come from the environment itself! Here are a few good suggestions for extending your reach—and that of your students—outside the classroom and into the real world.

#11-13
A to Zany, Community Activities for Students of English (1998) by Lynn Stafford-Yilmaz. Ann Arbor: University of Michigan Press. ISBN 0-472-08501-8. 185 pp., spiral-bound.

Use your community as a classroom! This book has many good ideas to get your students doing research on the culture around them. There are 26 chapters, each on a different topic, such as garage sales, newspapers, older adults and supermarkets. For each topic, there are several activities suggested, including going out in the community to make observations. Short written exercises and report forms help the students to focus their attention on specific points.

Some of these observation activities are for small groups, some for pairs and some can be done individually. You could incorporate one of these activities a week into your class, and have the students do the observations for homework. There are a lot of good ideas provided for follow-up activities. The material is best for intermediate or higher level students, but the ideas are adaptable to any level. AS: "I find this book really inspiring."

#11-14
Using the Newspaper to Teach Basic Living Skills (1988, 1998) by Jean Bunnell. Portland, ME: J. Weston Walch Publisher. ISBN 0-8251-3726-8. 133pp. Reproducible worksheets.

While not written specifically for ESL, the language level and content of this book is perfect for high-beginning or intermediate level ESL. There are 54 activities in which students are asked to search for certain kinds of information in a local paper. Good suggestions for follow-up discussion are given. For example, in Chapter 17, *What's the Pay?* students have to find five help-wanted ads that tell the hourly rate of pay; they note these on their worksheet. Next, the students have to work out the weekly and annual pay based on this, and note the results. Finally, the teacher brings in a federal withholding guide and helps students calculate payroll deductions. Discussion of state or city income taxes can follow this. Or look at Chapter 52, which has students use the sports pages to find out the home cities of basketball teams and mark them on a map!

One thing we like about this book is that unlike some lifeskills materials it is not condescending in tone—it is interesting and task-oriented. It's definitely worth having on your shelf.

See also:
The *Civic Participation* section in Chapter 10 (items #10-25, 26) for other ideas on involving your students in community life.

Other community resources: Free teaching materials

Many ESL teachers use print materials available in the surrounding community for English lessons. This gives the students a chance to learn useful vocabulary while also learning about the culture and what's available to them here. The following are a few ideas; you may get further ideas from your own community.

Supermarkets. Many supermarkets have a weekly flyer with sale items and coupons—great for basic vocabulary or cost comparisons. Some larger stores may have a floor map available—you could make a treasure hunt based on this. Ask the manager if they'll offer your students a tour of the store, and have the students prepare some questions ahead of time.

Advertising. Posters, billboards, announcements and other outdoor print can make interesting assignments. Have students add events that interest them to a class calendar.

Banks. Banks have brochures with information about different types of accounts. They also have forms.

Post office. The Post Office has a lot of forms (such as the *Change of Address* form) that your students could study and practice filling out. Many of these are important to know about. Tours for student groups are usually available if you ask.

Newspaper ads. Business advertisements for clothing, appliances, airfares and other items give students a chance to compare prices and features. Dates of sales, hours of business, addresses and phone numbers to call for more information all provide teaching material. Classified advertisements for cars, apartments, yard sales and jobs help familiarize the students with the community and the opportunities it offers. They also give the students a chance to make comparisons and to interpret and expand on abbreviated language.

Junk mail. Catalogs, ads for shopping, coupons and other unwanted mail can be integrated into units such as clothing, food, providing additional vocabulary and comparisons.

Medical centers. Doctors' offices and clinics often have free brochures about health issues. It's possible they also have lectures or speakers on issues of interest to your students. See if you can get a copy of any admission forms for your students to practice on.

Phone book. You might be able to pick up a class set of phone books at a recycling center, or ask the phone company if they still have some from a previous year to give away. There are many good classroom exercises you can do with these, including scanning, using the alphabet, locating names, addresses and phone numbers and locating information in the yellow pages.

Library. Any public library will be happy to arrange a tour for your students. They may even be willing to customize the tour to the students' interests. Most libraries have lots of free information you or your students can pick up. We like to encourage students to ask the librarians questions so that they realize what a helpful resource these people are.

School notices. If your students have children in school you have a rich resource for learning material. Schools routinely send monthly calendars of events to parents as well as notices of conferences and meetings, requests for information and permissions. Studying these is a way to encourage parents to participate more fully in their children's school community.

Multi-Media Resources

In this chapter we have grouped TV and video, computer and internet resources. Some of these are designed specifically for ESL classes while others are for the general public and can be adapted for your students. Some of these resources are for teacher reference.

TV and Video

#12-1

Video in Second Language Teaching: Using, Selecting and Producing Video for the Classroom (1992) by Susan Stempleski and Paul Acario, editors. Alexandria: Teachers of English to Speakers of Other Languages, Inc. 183pp. ISBN 0-939791-41-2.

This book gives concrete suggestions on integrating videos into the curriculum as well as suggestions for selecting videos. It also gives tips on making videos with students. It is clearly written and easy to use.

#12-2

Connect with English: A Video-Based Program (1998). Videos available from The Annenberg/CPB Collection, P.O. Box 2345, South Burlington, VT. 05407. 1-800-532-7637. Print materials are available from McGraw Hill (#13-22 in the *Publishers* section). These include *Video Comprehension Books* (with preview activities, comprehension and interpretation questions, discussion topics and other activities), *Conversation Books*, *Grammar Guides*, *Video Scripts* and sixteen *Graded Readers*. All of these come in four levels; there are instructor's manuals for most components.

Although it is suggested that these videos are appropriate for high beginning and intermediate classes, in most adult programs they would be suitable for high intermediate and up. The series follows a young woman from Boston who travels across the United States to San Francisco to study music. During her cross-country trip she encounters many people and the real problems and issues in their lives as well as in her own. The main character and her story are very engaging. Important cultural information is integrated into the story. Each episode is divided into shorter segments. After each segment, a group of ESL students recall important parts of the story and relate them to their own lives. The speech is natural and comprehensible. It is slightly slowed down and simplified but never to the point of sounding inauthentic. As in real life, there is sometimes background noise, which makes listening more challenging but not too difficult.

The videos with their accompanying printed texts provide more than enough material for a fully integrated course.

#12-3

Crossroads Café, K. Lynn Savage, Series Editor. Videos published by INTELE-COM, 150 E. Colorado Blvd. Suite 300, Pasadena, CA 91105-1937. Tel: 800-576-2988. Accompanying print materials published by Heinle & Heinle (#13-16 in the *Publishers* section). These include: Photo stories, worktexts, teacher's resource books, reproducible handouts and an assessment package, for both levels A and B. A *Partner Guide* is available for tutors. (Tip: All materials, both video and print, are also available from LVA, #13-21 in the *Publishers* section.)

The special feature of this video program is that it is designed for self-study. In places where the series is broadcast, students can view it at home and do workbook materials on their own. They can also work with a tutor, or the material can be used in a classroom setting.

The 26-part TV series is based on a continuing story centered in a restaurant. The main characters include immigrants and native speakers with a wide range of ethnicities and ages. Most of the speech is at native speed. Each episode is a half-hour in length but contains a lot of material. The story is complex, and sometimes seems a bit disconnected. It is less dramatic than the story in *Connect with English* and the language seems less authentic. Each video segment also includes word play and culture clips sections.

The workbook materials are well designed and provide just enough challenge to help students comprehend the story. The photo stories are nice and could be used to preview a segment, or to review it and retell or discuss an episode. The teacher's resource book gives detailed tips for classroom lessons. We especially like the handouts, which are student-centered and interesting. The series is most suitable for low intermediate and higher levels.

See also:

VIDIOMS (item #9-25 in the *Idioms* section) for an entertaining 3-tape set that teaches idioms in context.

Audio Forum (item #13-4 in the *Publishers* section), a source for video and audio programs.

Computer Skills and Computer Assisted Language Learning (CALL)

#12-4

E-mail for English Teaching (1995) by Mark Warschauer. Teachers of English to Speakers of Other Languages (TESOL), Inc. 120pp. ISBN 0-939791-62-5.

You may think that e-mail is something you need the internet for, but have you considered using it just within your classroom? Even if there's only one computer there, students can leave each other messages. What a motivating opportunity to practice writing! In Chapter 3 of this book, *E-mail in a Single Classroom* and in Chapter 4, *E-Mail for Cross-Cultural Exchange* you'll find some good teaching ideas for this type of activity. The rest of the book has more to do with using the internet.

See also:

Focus on Grammar (item #8-11 in the *Grammar* section) which has an interactive software program on CD-ROM to accompany the texts. Although we haven't reviewed this software, at least one teacher has told us her high intermediate students enjoy using the program.

#12-5

Keystrokes to Literacy, Using the Computer as a Learning Tool for Adult Beginning Readers (1991, 1996) by Antonia Stone. Lincolnwood: NTC/Contemporary. ISBN 0-8442-0679-2. 195pp, spiral-bound.

For students who have no familiarity with a computer at all, this book offers simple, fun-to-do exercises that will gradually introduce them to the concepts they need and will help them gain confidence and skill. You can do these with any kind of computer and no special software is needed except a word processor (later chapters also call for a database program, a spreadsheet and graphics program). Many teachers have recommended this book and with good reason— the author is clearly a master teacher who presents her lessons in just the right-sized segments to give the students a sense of accomplishment without frustrating them. Her tips and guidelines are very helpful.

After working through these exercises over a number of sessions, students should at least feel comfortable writing something independently on the computer and printing it out. What other skills they learn will depend on the students and the time available. This text is useful for tutoring as well as teaching groups.

See also:

The *Dictionaries* section (Chapter 9) for several dictionaries that come with CD-ROM programs.

Athelstan, Inc. (#13-3 in the *Publisher* section) for basic language learning software. Some of these are older, classic programs that are great for language activities.

Internet ESL

Even those adult programs that already have computers for their classrooms don't necessarily have internet hookups. As more and more schools and individuals get connected, though, the wealth of materials online for adult ESL students will expand. In the meantime, there are more and more teacher resources online that might enhance your classroom. Here are some resources to help you get started exploring.

Internet ESL: Books

#12-6

Dave Sperling's Internet Guide, Second Edition (1997, 1998) by Dave Sperling. Upper Saddle River: Prentice Hall Regents, now Pearson Education. 183pp. ISBN 0-13-918053-2.

If you are new to the internet or are just overwhelmed by it, this book can help you focus on what's available for ESL. There's an introduction to the internet with some helpful tips, a chapter on searching for information, a description of the many different ways teachers and students can communicate on the net, and a 45-page guide to the best of the Web for ESL teachers. (While these entries can also be found on the author's website, *Dave's ESL Café,* here they are annotated which is very helpful.) Finally, there is a section on looking for jobs on the internet.

Because things in cyberspace change quickly, it's possible some of the information in the book may be outdated, but you can locate an update on the author's website. There is so much good stuff here it will keep you busy for a long, long time.

#12-7

Internet Tasks for Second Language Students (1998) by David Cohn, Douglas E. Moore and Carmela Taliercio-Cohn. Elmont, NY: Proficiency Press Co. 52pp. ISBN 1-879279-16-9.

This reproducible book of structured, sheltered internet activities is useful to help your students gain familiarity and confidence using the Web. Each of the 13 units has a section that can be completed in about half an hour of online time; follow-up activities can be used at your discretion. For example, an activity on restaurants has the students visit three online restaurant sites and answer some questions about them. Follow-up activities include discussion, writing, and more web searching. The 'penpal' assignments are a good idea. The really neat feature of this book is that it is accompanied by its own website, where the students try out the internet tasks. Best for intermediate level and up.

Internet ESL: Websites

#12-8

Dave's ESL Café. This website, by the author of the Internet Guide (item #12-6 above), is the best starting place for ESL teachers looking for information on the internet. It has many interactive features for both students and teachers. Dave's Web Guide (with links to other sites on the internet) is massive and can seem overwhelming but there's a lot of good stuff there if you keep looking. AS: "This is where I send people when I don't know the answers to their questions." The address is: http://www.eslcafe.com

#12-9

Andreas Lund: English as Another Language. We love this warm and user-friendly website by a teacher in Norway. It is thorough but selective and frequently updated. Andreas has fewer links but you may find things here you didn't see on Dave's site. Look for his page of links to ready-made lessons, the tutorials for web searching you can use with your students and check out the grammar poetry! You can read and compose these online or use the idea in your classroom. The address is: http://home.sol.no/~anlun/

#12-10

TOPICS Magazine. This online magazine presented by Sandy and Thomas Peters is made up entirely of student writings. Students from all over the world contribute short pieces on a wide range of topics, including news events, cultural topics and personal stories. Many include color photos. Students can browse through the writings online, or teachers can print out and share selected pieces with the class. Students can also submit their own writing to be published on the site, and we think this is an exciting feature. The material may be best suited for high intermediate or advanced level students. In addition to providing lots of interesting reading material (for free!), it's also a great source of contemporary topics for student discussion and writing. See it at: http://www.rice.edu/projects/topics/Electronic/Magazine.html

Other Internet Resources

#12-11

The Ultimate Collection of News Links. If your students have access to a computer, they probably already know that they can read newspapers online in their first language. In many cases, there are also English-language newspapers from their home countries online. These could provide you and your students with reading and discussion material. To locate international newspapers, as well as papers within the U.S., try this site, which has over 10,000 newspapers and magazines organized by country. It's at: http://pppp.net/links/news/

#12-12

NIFL-ESL Listserv. This is an e-mail discussion forum for ESL/ESOL instructors, program directors, or anyone with interest in ESL literacy. It is sponsored by the National Institute for Literacy.

For questions on any issues not covered in this book (for example testing, funding, agencies, instruction specific to certain language groups, special needs or specific job training), or for any other related questions, try posting your question on this forum. Hundreds of ESL colleagues and literacy professionals read this every day, and you are likely to find someone who has an idea or a reference for you or an experience to share.

To post a message, you need to sign up first. Visit the NCLE website (see item #13-24 in the *Publishers* chapter) to find information on how to do this. The address is: http://www.cal.org/ncle

Publishers and Distributors

About Distributors

We generally prefer ordering books from a distributor when possible, as their service is fast (we've had good service from each of these companies) and you can order materials from more than one publisher at the same time. Their catalogs are a useful resource to have on your shelf because they carry helpful descriptions of each of the items, which allows you to compare similar books from different publishers. Not all publishers' books are available through distributors, so it is useful to get catalogs from the individual publishers as well. You may want to compare prices, since occasionally prices are slightly higher from a distributor.

All of these companies serve both schools and individuals. This is a quick-reference; see more detailed information listed in the individual entries below.

For ESL books and materials from many publishers, see:

- **Alta ESL Book Center Publishers** in Burlingame, California
  (1-800-ALTA/ESL) www.altaesl.com

- **Delta Systems Co., Inc.** in McHenry, Illinois
  (1-800-323-8270) www.delta-systems.com

- **Miller Educational Materials, Inc.** in Buena Park, California
  (1-800-636-4375) www.millereducational.com
  Specializes in materials from smaller publishers.

For computer software and technology, see:

- **Athelstan, Inc.** in Houston, Texas
  (1-800-598-3880) www.athel.com
  Specializes in language learning software, including ESL.

- **Educational Resources** in Elgin, Illinois
  (1-800-624-2926) www.edresources.com

Commercial educational software of all kinds and levels, not specifically for ESL learning.

Publishers and Distributors

Here is a list of 37 publishers and distributors who have materials of interest to adult ESL instructors and students, with addresses so you can request a catalog.

We have included web addresses also, although most publishers' web sites are still "in development"—that is to say not always helpful and sometimes confusing. As these things change rapidly, though, you may want to take a look anyway. Also, please note that web addresses sometimes change, so if the address we've given doesn't work, try a web search instead.

Note: Be sure to request the ESL catalog if that's what you need—some publishers, especially the larger ones, produce several catalogs for different purposes.

#13-1
Addison Wesley Longman (now a division of Pearson Education)
1 Jacob Way
Reading, MA 01867 USA
Internet: www.awl.com

Orders go to Pearson Education (#13-29 below).

Addison Wesley Longman (now part of Pearson Education) has published a useful collection of materials for ESL students at every level. We love their learner's dictionaries for intermediate and advanced students. They have some fine reading textbooks and many "readers"—stories in paperback form for pleasure reading. The *Longman Pilgrims* series is a well-known and useful teacher resource. Their website (as of this writing) included detailed information about each title—to find this, go to the 'Online Store' first and use the search feature there.

All of their available titles appear in the Pearson Education ESL catalog as well as on the Pearson website.

#13-2
Alta Book Center Publishers
14 Adrian Court
Burlingame, CA 94010 USA
Internet: www.altaesl.com
1-800-ALTA/ESL

Alta publishes a growing list of classroom-ready ESL materials and teacher resources (including this book!). They have republished some of the practical classics in our field such as *Action English Pictures* and *Drawing Out* as well.

Alta is also a distributor for ESL materials of all kinds from many publishers. Their large catalog is especially helpful because it indicates which titles are useful for adults. Alta's website includes an online catalog you can browse through or search.

#13-3
Athelstan, Inc.
2476 Bolsover St #464
Houston, TX 77005-2518 USA
Internet: www.athel.com
1-800-598-3880

Athelstan is a distributor of computer software program and CD-ROMs for second language learning. These include teacher 'authoring programs' in which you can enter your own text for students to work on. Your best bet is to visit their web site and look for the ESL section. Each title is described in detail online.

#13-4
Audio-Forum
96 Broad St
Guilford, CT 06437-2612 USA
Internet: www.audioforum.com
1-800-243-1234

Audio-Forum, a distributor of audio and video language courses, now has an ESL catalog. They carry materials you can't find anywhere else, such as bilingual survival courses for speakers of Chinese, Khmer, Lao, Spanish, Vietnamese, etc. These might be useful for self-study. Videos of possible interest include some travel guides to sites in the U.S. and Canada, and interview programs about the life of an immigrant family for three generations (this is available for 14 different cultures). If you want to learn a foreign language yourself, ask for their *Whole World* catalog, which lists courses for 101 languages.

#13-5
Cambridge University Press
40 West 20th St
New York, NY 10011 USA
Internet: www.cup.org
1-800-872-7423

Cambridge University Press is best known for its series of ESL Teacher Resource/Handbook/Training materials, but for classroom use they also carry some practical listening and pronunciation texts of high quality. For intermediate or advanced ESL students needing Business English, they have quite a few selections. You can browse, search and order from their website—select ESL/EFL at the top of the main page.

#13-6
Delta Systems Co., Inc.
1400 Miller Parkway
McHenry, IL 60050-7030 USA
Internet: www.delta-systems.com
1-800-323-8270

Delta publishes the Center for Applied Linguistics (CAL) titles in the field of adult literacy education, and a growing number of useful adult ESL titles. Their large catalog describes ESL books and materials from many different publishers and is a must for your resource shelf. Their website has a good search engine. You can search for a specific item, or browse by selecting a category on the search page.

#13-7
Dominie Press, Inc.
1949 Kellogg Avenue
Carlsbad, CA 92008 USA
Internet: www.dominie.com
1-800-232-4570

Dominie Press is a good source for collections of folktales and stories from around the world, both for adults and for kids. They also have some literacy-level texts for adult ESL, some new workplace ESL materials, as well as a few important professional development titles. Many of their texts are suitable for young adults in a school setting. You can order a catalog from their website.

#13-8
Educational Resources
1550 Executive Dr., P.O. Box 1900
Elgin, IL 60121-1900 USA
Internet: www.edresources.com
1-800-624-2926

Educational Resources is a distributor of software and all kinds of useful classroom technology. They don't have specific ESL teaching software, but they have many general items that are useful for ESL, including: word processors, utility programs, graphics programs, game software, K-12 learning software (some of which can be used with adult students), science programs, authoring software for teachers, keyboarding programs and hardware. Their prices are competitive and they ship both to individuals and to schools.

#13-9
ELT Technical Assistance Project
Spring Institute for International Studies
1610 Emerson St
Denver, CO 80218 USA
Internet: www.springinstitute.com/elt
303-863-0188

ELT is a project sponsored in part by the U.S. Office of Refugee Resettlement to provide technical assistance to programs serving refugee students. They have published a number of excellent articles that are clear, practical and directly useful in the classroom. For example, *ABC's for Tutors: 26 Teaching Tips* is so useful you'll want to laminate your copy! Other articles specifically address the workplace SCANS skills with useful teaching tips. These materials are available free of charge for downloading on the ELT website, or you can request an article by mail.

#13-10
Excellence in Education Publications
300 North Stadium Dr
Monmouth, OR 97361 USA
1-800-852-0969

They publish just a few titles, some with tapes, suitable for adult ESL. Prices are reasonable, especially if you order class sets.

#13-11
Full Blast Productions
P.O. Box 1297
Lewiston, NY 14092-8297 USA
(in Canada: Box 408, Virgil, Ontario, L0S 1T0)
Internet: www.fullblastproductions.com
905-468-7558

Full Blast Productions has a video for teaching idioms called *VIDIOMS* which is great if you can get your program to invest in it. They have puzzle books and a number of texts with short readings on cultural themes, international holidays, etc. Their "jigsaw" materials for small group work look interesting, too.

#13-12
Glencoe (a division of McGraw Hill)
P.O. Box 508
Columbus, OH 43216 USA
Internet: www.glencoe.com
1-800-334-7344

Glencoe isn't specifically for ESL materials, but they have workplace and vocational materials (in a Career Ed catalog) that might be useful for ESL students, and their high school Social Studies catalog has civics texts about U.S.

government that might be interesting and useful for supplementing your citizenship courses. Their *American Humanities Resource Package* (history of American music, art, crafts, games) looks interesting and possibly adaptable to ESL.

#13-13
Globe Fearon
4350 Equity Dr
P.O. Box 2649
Columbus, OH 43216 USA
Internet: www.globefearon.com
1-800-848-9500

Globe Fearon isn't an ESL publisher! They do publish ABE materials in all subject areas and lifeskills materials, many of which might be adaptable for your ESL students. For example, some of the Social Studies titles would be useful for civics lessons. A series of resource binders called *Lifeschool 2000* provides ideas for teaching health and consumer topics. Also of interest is their long list of graded readers—these low-level readers, such as the *Fastbacks* series, are short novels with adult content which would be very useful for your ESL students' pleasure reading. (Their website is great—go to the 'Teacher's Room' and check out the links pages for adult education!)

#13-14
Hands-on English
P.O. Box 256
Crete, NE 68333 USA
Internet: www.handsonenglish.com
1-800-375-4263

Hands-on English is a newsletter-style publication that comes out six times a year, specifically for teachers of adult ESL. Each issue includes reproducible activities, puzzles and useful ideas for the classroom, some contributed by readers. The website has additional ready-to-use activities on current events. No catalog, but a free sample issue will be sent on request.

#13-15
Harcourt Brace and Company, College Division
6277 Sea Harbor Dr
Orlando, FL 32887 USA
Internet: www.harcourt.com
1-800-245-8744

Unfortunately, Harcourt no longer publishes an ESL catalog. We include this information here because they publish a few good ESL titles that are useful for adult students, although they are listed in the company's College Division. Their website is frustrating, their phone ordering confusing; you'll be happier if you can avoid doing business with this company. Fortunately some, though not all, of the ESL titles are available from Steck-Vaughn (see item #13-34).

#13-16
Heinle & Heinle Publishers
20 Park Plaza
Boston, MA 02116 USA
Internet: www.heinle.com
1-800-278-2574

Heinle & Heinle has a huge catalog with useful materials for every level of ESL from middle school to adult to university, low beginning through advanced academic. They also publish the written materials for the *Crossroads Café* television/video series. Their catalog is detailed with charts to help you see which materials will work for which students. There is also complete information about each title on the website.

#13-17
Houghton Mifflin College Division
222 Berkeley St
Boston, MA 02116
Internet: www.hmco.com/college/esl
1-800-854-8454

Houghton Mifflin has a relatively small collection of ESL texts, mostly appropriate for higher level students. They also publish the *Amazing Stories* readers, and many high quality dictionaries. Their website is friendly and they have a nice online ESL catalog.

#13-18
Intercultural Press
PO Box 700
Yarmouth, ME 04096 USA
Internet: www.interculturalpress.com
1-800-370-2665

Intercultural Press does not offer ESL instruction books, but rather they publish and distribute books and videos about cross-cultural communication. Some of these might be useful for ESL teachers, such as books on understanding cultural differences and interesting titles on specific cultures such as Mexican, Chinese, Filipino, Japanese, etc. Quite a few titles offer help for those planning to live and work overseas. Some titles are specifically for business and training. Many of their titles are difficult to find elsewhere. They publish a detailed catalog several times a year.

#13-19
JAG Publications
11288 Ventura Blvd., Suite 301
Studio City, CA 91604 USA
Internet: www.jagpublications-esl.com/
818-505-9002

JAG Publications is a small publisher with a few titles of interest to adult ESL, including *Comics and Conversation*, a book of uncaptioned cartoons for students to talk or write about.

#13-20
Linmore Publishing, Inc.
P.O. Box 1545
Palatine, IL 60078 USA
1-800-336-3656
Internet: www.linmore.com

Linmore Publishing is a small "teachers' press" that has a number of books useful for ESL literacy students and beginners. *Stories from the Heart* and other titles offer authentic stories written by adult ESL students. The website is helpful and gives full information about each title. Orders for individual titles are faster through a distributor; school orders can go directly to Linmore. They give quantity discounts.

#13-21
Literacy Volunteers of America (LVA)
635 James St
Syracuse, NY 13203 USA
Internet: www.literacyvolunteers.org
1-800-LVA-8812

LVA is a non-profit organization that has support materials for basic reading tutors and ESL tutors, as well as some real gems on managing literacy programs, including a workplace education guide and a community relations guide. Look here for family literacy materials, and a Learning Disabilities Digest. LVA also carries video materials for both students and instructors.

Longman titles: see Pearson Education (item **#13-29** below).

#13-22
McGraw-Hill Higher Education/ESOL
Two Penn Plaza, 20th Floor
New York, NY 10121-2298 USA
Internet: www.mhhe.com
1-800-624-7294

McGraw-Hill has several ESL course series which might be useful in adult ESL programs. They also have a new video-based program called *Connect with English* that includes course texts and graded readers. We like *Sing It!*, a six-level supplementary text, with audio cassette tapes, that teaches grammar and vocabulary through songs of all kinds. To locate these and other materials for adult students on their website, select "ESOL" under "Discipline" on the main page.

#13-23
Miller Educational Materials, Inc.
7300 Artesia Blvd
Buena Park, CA 90621 USA
Internet: www.millereducational.com
1-800-636-4375

This distributor of ESL materials includes many titles from smaller publishers that are hard to find, as well as a good selection of more well-known titles. The catalog has K-12 and Adult materials mixed together. Some non-ESL materials that are nonetheless useful are included, as well as posters, maps, great visuals and other classroom items. If you're looking for short readers for free reading you'll find about a zillion of them here.

#13-24
National Clearinghouse for ESL Literacy Education (NCLE)
Center for Applied Linguistics (CAL)
4646 40th St NW
Washington, DC 20016-1859 USA
Internet: www.cal.org/ncle
202-362-0700, ext 200

NCLE is a program with funding from the U.S. Department of Education that has provided services to adult ESL educators since 1990. They publish over 60 articles, called 'ERIC Digests,' on adult ESL teaching and policy issues that provide a valuable overview and references for further research. For example, *Teaching Multilevel Adult ESL Classes* briefly describes strategies and techniques that are known to succeed in this setting.

These articles are available free upon request, or you can download them yourself from the NCLE website. NCLE has other materials and information as well, including *NCLE Notes*, a twice-yearly newsletter. We think their workplace education resources are especially helpful. The website has an especially useful links page for resources on literacy and adult education issues.

#13-25
NTC/Contemporary Publishing Company
4255 West Touhy Ave
Lincolnwood, IL 60712 USA
Internet: www.ntc-cb.com
1-800-323-4900

NTC/Contemporary is a group that combines: National Textbook Company, Contemporary Books and Jamestown Publishers. They have some citizenship materials, GED texts, many workplace and lifeskills titles, some bilingual dictionaries and teacher resources. *English, Yes!* is a seven-level series that teaches English through literature, which might be of interest to young adults.

#13-26
New Readers Press
P.O. Box 888
Syracuse, NY 13210-0888 USA
Internet: www.newreaderspress.com
1-800-448-8878

New Readers Press, the publishing division of the non-profit Laubach Literacy, publishes the *LifePrints* series, a valuable three-level text for beginning students that combines language learning with lifeskills themes. They also carry workplace literacy materials, low-level readers in the *Writers' Voices* series, and *News for You*, an easy-reading adult newspaper that advanced ESL students can benefit from.

#13-27
Optima Books
2820 Eighth St
Berkeley, CA 94710
Internet: www.optimabooks.com
1-877-710-2196

Optima publishes several titles on slang and idioms, including the *Street Talk* series, *Biz Talk*, and several reference books. The slang books are probably of greatest interest to younger adults or teens.

#13-28
Oxford University Press
198 Madison Ave
New York, NY 10016-4314 USA
Internet: www.oup-usa.org/esl
1-800-451-7556

Oxford University Press publishes the four-part *Crossroads* textbook series (especially good for low-beginners), and the well-known *Oxford Picture Dictionary* materials. Their text dictionaries are also very high quality. No ESL teacher should be without the *Jazz Chants* books—there are three that are suitable for adults. Oxford also publishes some graded readers that would be great for a pleasure reading collection. Their professional titles are some of the best in the business.

#13-29
Pearson Education
ESL Adult & Higher Education
10 Bank Street, 9th Floor
White Plains, NY 10606-1951
1-800-282-0693 (individual orders)
1-800-922-0579 (school orders)
1-800-266-8855 (ESL help desk)

Internet: www.pearsoned-elt.com

This company has merged Addison Wesley Longman and Prentice Hall Regents (along with Scott Foresman and Simon & Shuster) into one big company. Ask for their *ESL Adult and Higher Education Catalog*, which includes all available ESL titles by these publishers. Their website includes an online catalog. If you wish to order any of their titles, however, you'll get better service ordering from one of the ESL distributors listed above.

#13-30
Pippin Publishing Corp.
85 Ellesmere Rd, Suite 232
Scarsborough, Ontario M1R 4B9, CANADA
Email: jld@pippinpub.com
1-888-889-0001

Pippin's collection includes ESL titles about teaching both children and adults. Their *Pippin Teacher's Library* series includes several titles specifically about classroom issues in teaching adults. (In the U.S. this professional education series is available through the Wright Group in Bothell, Washington, 1-800-523-2371).

Pippin also has some practical classroom activity books such as *Decisions* (a problem-solving text). In the U.S. these titles are available either through distributors or directly from the publisher. Pippin is especially notable for their titles about Canadian history and culture.

#13-31
Prentice Hall Regents (now a division of Pearson Education)
200 Old Tappan Rd
Old Tappan, NJ 07675 USA
Internet: www.phregents.com

Orders go to Pearson Education (item #13-29 above).

Prentice Hall Regents (now part of Pearson Education) has published some of the most-used grammar texts, including the Azar series and the Breyer series, among others. They have also published wonderful beginning-level reading texts, some citizenship materials and useful teacher resources such as the reproducible picture story books. Their website, as of this writing, had detailed descriptions of some of the books and sample pages in some cases.

All of their available titles appear in the Pearson Education ESL catalog as well as on the Pearson website.

#13-32
Pro Lingua Associates
15 Elm St
Brattleboro, VT 05301 USA
Internet: www.ProLinguaAssociates.com
1-800-366-4775

Pro Lingua Associates is a small independent publisher with a high proportion of useful materials. Some of their titles are just plain classics that every ESL teacher should have, such as the *Index Card Games* and *Conversation Inspirations*. You'll find story cards and puzzle books here also. Their website includes book reviews of many of their titles.

#13-33
Proficiency Press Co.
18 Lucille Ave
Elmont, NY 11003
Internet: www.ProficiencyPress.com
212-928-7002

This small company publishes practical titles for foreign language teachers and has only two titles for ESL so far. One of these is the useful and innovative *Internet Tasks for Second Language Students*.

#13-34
Steck-Vaughn (a division of Harcourt Brace & Co.)
P.O. Box 26015
Austin, TX 78755
Internet: www.steck-vaughn.com
1-800-531-5015

In the past Steck-Vaughn has had mostly GED and mainstream Adult Ed materials. Recently they published *English ASAP*, a nice beginning series for ESL students in the workplace. They also have an ESL citizenship text and a number of civics titles which might also be adaptable to ESL students. Some of their graded readers with adult content (such as the *Great Unsolved Mysteries* series) might be used for ESL students' pleasure reading. Their *Adult Education* catalog also includes some of the Harcourt Brace/Holt Rinehart Winston ESL titles that can be hard to find.

#13-35
Teachers of English to Speakers of Other Languages (TESOL), Inc.
700 S Washington St, Suite 200
Alexandria, VA 22314
Internet: www.tesol.edu
Office: 703-836-0774
Publications: 1-888-891-0041

TESOL, the professional organization for ESL teachers, has a growing list of publications. Some of these are professional titles such as the *Directory of TESOL Programs*, but others are about practical teaching ideas, such as their *New Ways* series.

#13-36
University of Michigan Press
P.O. Box 1104
Ann Arbor, MI 48106-1104
Internet: www.press.umich.edu/esl
Orders: 734-764-4392

This publisher's ESL titles are mostly appropriate for academic settings. They do have pre-academic materials, though, as well as business titles, a text on medical English and materials for International Teaching Assistants (ITA's). More recently they have published some practical texts of interest to adult ESL, including *A to Zany*.

#13-37
J. Weston Walch Publisher
P.O. Box 658
Portland, ME 04104-0658
Internet: www.walch.com
1-800-341-6094

This publisher has imaginative texts for mainstream high school and adult teaching, as well as a few titles specifically for ESL, including a citizenship text. Some of the mainstream materials might also be adaptable to adult ESL, including the lifeskills text on cars and driving and one called *Read that Label!* The *Super Reader* series of short stories like *Amazing Rescues* written at grade level 6 could be part of an ESL pleasure reading collection. They have lots of multicultural biographies and texts, including some on consumer math. They have a good online catalog.

A Shopper's Guide to Jargon

We have tried to write this book in the most 'jargon-free' manner possible, so that it is accessible to anyone working with ESL students, no matter what their background or training. Certain terms do come up frequently however—sometimes in the titles of the books themselves! Most of these terms describe approaches to teaching. We thought it would be helpful to clarify these here.

To illustrate the terms below, we've chosen the example of a lesson on *using the telephone*. This should help you compare the approaches more easily.

Communicative instruction

Students practice real communication during the course of the lesson. For example, using play phones they call each other up to talk or ask a question. Or, as a homework assignment they call a classmate on the phone from home.

This approach helps students learn the language through the need to communicate in the workplace and in the community. On the other hand, because the emphasis is on communication rather than on correctness, students may form poor language habits.

Competency-based instruction

A 'competency' is a specific task which the student learns how to complete. For example, taking a phone message or calling in sick.

Many competency programs have checklists so the students can mark off what they've learned and can see what they've accomplished. This is very satisfying, both to students and teachers. Because this approach seems to give immediate results, it is often seen in workplace programs. One weakness is the need to provide many, many instructions on how to do things; it can be very teacher-centered. And like *survival skills* (below), when used alone this approach may fail to provide a strong language learning background.

Context-based instruction, contextualized instruction

A *context* for a lesson is ideally a story, or at the least a situation. For example, the students might hear or read a story about a misunderstanding someone (such as a fellow student) had when they made an important telephone call. This story is then used as a basis for language learning.

This approach, when used as the starting point for instruction, has the potential of bringing all the other approaches together under one roof. Beware, though, that this term has become very trendy and is sometimes used misleadingly by publishers; the label *contextualized* sometimes just means that some real-life examples are provided, which is not the same thing.

Cooperative learning approach

In this approach students learn in small groups, in which they are accountable for each others' learning. They have a specific group task and are to help each other succeed at it. Each member brings different information to the group. This kind of activity can be carefully structured, so that each student is assigned a specific task or role, such as timekeeper, recorder or reporter. For example, the teacher might give each student in a group a word or phrase on a piece of paper, which that student has to teach to the other members of the group. The group then must combine these into the text of a telephone conversation, which is written down and handed in.

Similarly, in *collaborative* learning students work together to complete a task, but the tasks and roles of the students may be somewhat less formally structured. For example, each group might be assigned to write and present a skit about calling the doctor's office. Students choose roles, plan the dialogue, write it down, practice it and then present it to the class.

In both cases the advantage over a traditional classroom structure is that the students are using a lot of their language skills in the process of negotiating to complete the task.

Functional approach, functional/notional approach

A *function* is an idea such as thanking, complaining, inviting, apologizing. This approach seeks to teach students varying ways of expressing these ideas with different levels of appropriacy (or register) depending on the situation. For example, students might learn some phrases to use when making a complaint, then given an example situation (i.e., you bought something that is defective) they practice making a phone call to complain.

This approach is found more commonly in overseas (EFL) teaching. It can be a little complicated to present and may be most appropriate for advanced level ESL students.

Grammar-based instruction

The teacher introduces a grammar concept (the sentence structure of a question, for example) and the students practice it in class. They might practice forming questions, for instance, then use them in telephone dialogues ("Would you like to. . . ?")

Students sometimes appreciate grammar-based instruction because, at the lower levels anyway, it is fairly concrete and learnable. One weakness is that, unless the practice examples are extremely carefully chosen and well-presented, student success in a grammar lesson does not often carry over into their real-life English use. In other words, it may be a waste of time. An alternative to this approach is to base the lessons on a *communicative, student-centered,* or *context-based* approach, but supply grammar lessons as needed when questions come up.

Integrated skills approach

An *integrated* approach (called a *four skills* approach in some texts) means that the four main language skills—speaking, listening, reading and writing—are all included in one lesson. For example, students might hear a tape of a telephone conversation, then try to re-tell what was said. Later they would read a copy of the text, perhaps write a dictation or a follow-up letter, then try making a similar telephone call themselves.

There are two good reasons for this approach—one is that some students learn better through listening and some through reading, etc., so you are providing the greatest amount of useful input. The other reason is that the different skills reinforce each other—what you learned by listening sinks in better after you've also read about it, and so on. It is well accepted in the field that almost any lesson benefits from an integrated approach.

Interactive instruction

Interactive usually just means that during the lesson the students do at least some activities with each other, either in pairs or small groups. For example, beginners might interview each other and take down each other's phone numbers (practicing listening and speaking at the same time). Or, higher level students in a small group might work together to generate a list of situations in which they need to use the telephone, providing discussion material for the class.

The idea is that students learn better by participating, and they get more actual speaking time than they would if the teacher called on each student individually. One weakness of this approach is that it can seem very diffuse to the learners, especially if they have expectations of a more *teacher-centered* approach. Although most teachers like interactive activities, they have to learn to justify their use to the students, making the goals clear.

Participatory approach

See *problem posing* on the next page.

Performance-based instruction

Like *competency-based* instruction and *survival skills* instruction, this approach seeks to teach beginning-level students what they will really need to know. Used in connection with literacy, it means students will start by learning important sight words (like FIRE, POLICE) and numeracy skills (such as reading and writing down phone numbers) that will allow them to take care of personal and work responsibilities. The next stage is 'communicative competence' which means that students will learn how to express the things they most need to say.

This approach is more *student-centered* than the other two approaches mentioned. It seeks to give the students some immediate success, while working on decoding skills and communication skills that will lead to more developed language later.

Problem-posing approach

In this activist approach, students explore real problems that they are facing, at work, at home or in the community, and try to find and implement solutions. For example, students who live in an apartment complex might explore the availability of public telephones and try to work with the management to make these more available. A language lesson would seek to give them the skills, vocabulary and strategies they need to do this.

This approach, based on the work of Paulo Freire in Brazil, assumes that adult students have critical concerns in their communities and that they may wish to take action to change things.

SCANS-based instruction

SCANS is a series of guidelines established by the U.S. Department of Labor in the early 1990's (it stands for Secretary of Labor's Commission on Achieving Necessary Skills). It is a list of behaviors, strategies and skills thought to affect a worker's success in the modern workplace.

In a nutshell, *SCANS* classroom instruction prepares students to solve problems they may encounter in the workplace. For example, what do you do if you can't understand what someone is saying to you on the phone? Students learn vital strategies (for example, asking for clarification) and practice them in class.

This approach may be more complex and harder for the instructor to grasp than teaching specific competencies, but in the long run it is very beneficial to the students. It gives them tools they can use in many different situations.

Student-centered instruction

The teacher bases the content of the lesson on the needs of his or her particular students. For example, the students list what kinds of problems they have had using the phone (calling their child's school, for example) and the teacher designs a lesson to help them with this.

The term *student-centered* is a popular one and is sometimes used misleadingly. Giving the students a chance to talk is not the same thing as giving them control over some of the content of the lesson.

Survival skills/lifeskills instruction

Teaches students how to deal with the most immediate necessities of life. How to call 9-1-1, for example, or perhaps how to use the phone directory.

This approach can be vitally important to newcomers. It often focuses on vocabulary as its main goal. It tends to be short-term and does not always seek to give the students a foundation for language learning, which they will need if they wish to progress further in English.

Task-based instruction

This can mean two things: Either the same as *competency-based*, above (students learn to complete certain tasks), or that certain classroom tasks are used to practice language skills (for example, an information-gap exercise or a puzzle the students have to solve). An example of the latter would be: Students have to telephone three restaurants to find out when they are open for business.

Teacher-centered instruction

Teacher-centered has become a kind of negative epithet, implying that the teacher: a) decides what the students need to learn, b) decides what they already know or don't know, c) decides what material to present, d) presents the material and expects the students to listen and learn. Of course, by definition most classrooms are teacher-centered, and many textbooks are as well.

Because a great deal of research and theory says that students learn better the more they participate (active rather than passive learning), many teachers (including these authors) look for ways to make their classrooms more *student-centered*. This does not mean abandoning the leadership role, however.

TPR (Total Physical Response)

This approach seeks to get students actively involved even at the very beginning levels by having them respond non-verbally to language they hear. For example, the teacher might tell a story ("Susanna called her sister on the telephone . . .") and ask the students to pantomime the story as they listen.

TPR can be integrated into any kind of lesson, and as a preliminary stage is a good way to ensure comprehension (listening and reading) before asking students to produce new language themselves (speaking and writing).

Whole language instruction

The idea of whole language is simply that meaning comes first and foremost, and the other language skills follow. It is similar to the *context-based* approach in that all language skills are learned together with the focus on a particular theme or topic. In a lesson, students might focus on the overall topic of using the telephone, including making calls, writing about their own experiences and sharing what they have written.

The *whole language* approach integrates language skills and provides plenty of opportunities for repetition and revisiting material. It stresses communication over correctness, with the assumption that correctness will come with time.

A Teaching Note

Finally, we'd like to say that no one approach is ever the answer to how to teach ESL. A good lesson would include several of these approaches in the same session, chosen according to the needs of the students and their learning styles. Knowing how to do this is what makes teaching not only a science, but also a craft.

Index

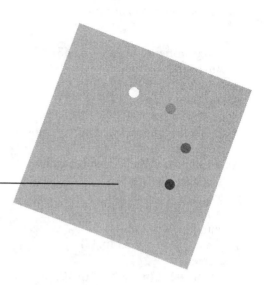

1,000 Pictures for Teachers to Copy
#4-19 (p.36)
10 Steps #7-12 (p.80)

A

A to Zany #11-13 (p.124)
"ABC's for Tutors," article cited in
#13-9 (p.137)
Abraham, Paul #5-39 (p.57), #6-18
(p.67)
Acario, Paul, editor #12-1 (p.127)
Ackert, Patricia #6-7 (p.64)
Action English Pictures #4-21 (p.37)
Action Plans #4-1 (p.30)
activities. *See* Chapter 4 (pp.29–42).
See also collaborative instruction,
communicative instruction; cooperative learning; discussion; humanistic
instruction; information gap; integrated approach; interactive instruction; multilevel classes; process
writing; problem posing; roleplay;
self access; sensory; simulation;
TPR; warmups. *See also* under each
level.
Adelman, Mara B. #11-3 (p.120)
Adelson-Goldstein, Jayme #5-28 (p.53),
#9-5 (p.94)
"Adult Literacy Training," article #3-1
(p.22)

adult students
characteristics of, #1-4 (p.8), #1-5
(p.9), #1-7 (p.9), #4-9 (p.32)
advanced level
activities for, #4-9 (p.32), #4-16
(p.35), #5-3 (p.44), #5-4 (p.44),
#5-12 (p.47), #5-14 (p.48), #6-1
(p.62), #7-3 (p.77)
description of, *see* Introduction (p.1)
grammar for, #8-8 (p.86), #8-16
(p.90)
reading texts for, #6-26 (p.70), #6-27
(p.71), #6-28 (p.71), #11-2
(p.120), #11-8 (p.123), #11-12
(p.124), #12-10 (p.131)
texts & coursebooks for, #5-11
(p.47), #5-13 (p.47), #5-27
(p.52), #5-33 (p.54), #5-45
(p.59), #7-8 (p.78), #7-10 (p.79),
#7-14 (p.81), #9-15 (p.98), #9-16
(p.98), #10-6 (p.109), #10-9
(p.110), #10-11 (p.111), #11-5
(p.121), #11-13 (p.124)
See also TOEFL preparation
Agendas for Second Language Literacy
#3-2 (p.22)
All Clear! Idioms in Context #9-22
(p.101)
All Clear! Intro #5-7 (p.45)
All Sides of the Issue #5-8 (p.46)

Amazing Stories series #6-4 (p.63),
   #6-16 (p.67)
America's Story #11-1 (p.119)
American Holidays #11-9 (p.123)
American Voices #11-2 (p.120)
Andreas Lund: English as Another Language website #12-9 (p.131)
*Approaches and Methods in Language
   Teaching* #1-1 (p.8)
*Approaches to Adult ESL Literacy In-
   struction* #3-3 (p.22)
Arthur, Lois #5-2 (p.44)
Ashkenas, Joan #4-23 (p.37)
assessment
   about, #1-2 (p.8), #1-9 (p.10), #1-19
      (p.12), #1-22 (p.13), #3-6 (p.23),
      #5-5 (p.45)
   alternative, #1-24 (p.13)
   of student needs, #1-4 (p.8)
Auerbach, Elsa Roberts #1-24 (p.13),
   #10-6 (p.109)
Azar, Betty Schrampfer #8-16 (p.90)

B
Back and Forth #4-2 (p.30)
Baker, Ann #5-43 (p.58)
Barnard, Roger #5-25 (p.52)
Basic Oxford Picture Dictionary #9-1
   (p.92)
*Basic Oxford Picture Dictionary Literacy
   Program* #3-4 (p.22)
Basic Tactics for Listening #5-23 (p.51)
Basic Vocabulary Builder series #9-17
   (p.99)
Bassano, Sharron #1-11 (p.11), #3-11
   (p.25), #4-4 (p.31), #4-13 (p.34)
Baudoin, E. Margaret #6-28 (p.71)
Becijos, Jeanne B. #6-24 (p.70)
Becker, Aliza #10-15 (p.113)
*Beginner's Dictionary of American Eng-
   lish Usage* #9-7 (p.95)
Beginners #3-5 (p.23)
Beginning Interactive Grammar #8-9
   (p.86)
beginning level
   activities & exercises for, #4-2 (p.30),
      #4-3 (p.30), #4-4 (p.31), #4-7
      (p.32), #4-8 (p.32), #4-11 (p.33),
      #4-12 (p.34), #4-18 (p.36), #4-22

(p.37), #4-25 (p.38), #4-28 (p.39),
   #4-30 (p.39), #4-31 (p.40), #4-36
   (p.41), #5-9 (p.46), #5-24 (p.51),
   #5-28 (p.53), #5-30 (p.53), #5-40
   (p.57), #8-3 (p.85), #8-15 (p.89)
description of, *see* Introduction (p.1),
   #3-5 (p.23)
how to teach, #1-6 (p.9), #3-5
   (p.23), #3-11 (p.25)
pictures & picture stories for, #4-21
   (p.37), #5-15 (p.48), #6-6 (p.64),
   #9-1 (p.92), #9-2 (p.92), #9-3
   (p.93), #9-17 (p.99), #9-18 (p.99),
   #9-19 (p.100)
stories & readings for, #6-4 through
   #6-15 (pp.63–66)
texts & coursebooks for, #2-1 (p.16),
   #2-2 (p.17), #2-3 (p.17), #2-4
   (p.18) #2-5 (p.19), #2-6 (p.20),
   #3-11 (p.25), #3-14 (p.27), #5-7
   (p.45), #5-10 (p.46), #7-12 (p.80),
   #7-13 (p.81), #8-9 (p.86), #8-10
   (p.87), #8-14 (p.88), #10-1
   (p.106), #10-2 (p.107), #10-4
   (p.108), #10-5 (p.108), #10-7
   (p.109)
beginning teachers. *See* new teachers
Beisbier, Beverly #5-46 (p.59)
Bell, Jill #1-9 (p.10), #3-7 (p.23)
Benson, Bryan #4-18 (p.36)
Berish, Lynda #6-4 (p.63), #6-16 (p.67)
Bernstein, Vivian #11-1 (p.119)
Betteridge, David #4-6 (p.32)
Beyond Language #11-3 (p.120)
bilingual materials #9-1 (p.92), #9-2
   (p.92), #9-3 (p.93), #9-5 (p.94),
   #13-2 (p.134), #13-4 (p.135),
   #13-23 (p.141), #13-25 (p.141)
   See also Spanish language materials
Bingo game #4-28 (p.39)
Blanchard, Karen #6-21 (p.68)
Blanton, Linda Lonan #7-8 (p.78)
Blass, Laurie #7-10 (p.79)
Bliss, Bill #10-4 (p.108), #10-23
   (p.116)
Blot, David #7-9 (p.79), #7-13 (p.81)
Bonner, Margaret #8-11 (p.87)
Book One #5-24 (p.51)
Boyd, John R. #5-24 (p.51)

Boyd, Mary Ann #5-24 (p.51)
Breyer, Pamela Peterson #8-13 (p.88)
Bringing Literacy to Life #3-6 (p.23)
Brinkman, Karen #3-16 (p.27)
Brinson, Boone #4-24 (p.38)
Brod, Shirley #3-4 (p.22), #3-8 (p.24)
Brookes, Gay #7-12 (p.80)
Broukal, Milada #11-6 (p.122)
Brown, H. Douglas #1-7 (p.9)
Brown, Ruthanne #4-8 (p.32)
Bruder, Mary Newton #5-17 (p.49)
Buckby, Michael #4-6 (p.32)
Building Real Life English Skills #6-17 (p.67)
Bunnell, Jean #11-14 (p.125)
Burke, David #9-15 (p.98)
Burnaby, Barbara #3-7 (p.23)
Burns, Anne #5-5 (p.45)
By the People, For the People #10-13 (p.112)
Byrne, Donn #1-21 (p.13)
Byrne, Mary Lou #10-10 (p.110)

C

Canada. *See* culture, Canadian
Card Book, The #4-22 (p.37)
Caring and Sharing #1-10 (p.10)
Carver, Tina Kasloff #5-10 (p.46)
Cason, Ann #1-25 (p.14)
Cathy's Cards #5-9 (p.46)
CD-ROMs. *See* computer software
Celce-Murcia, Marianne #8-2 (p.84), #8-8 (p.86), editor #1-8 (p.10)
Celebrate with Us #11-10 (p.123)
Chabot, John F. #4-36 (p.41), #9-25 (p.103)
Chalk Talks #5-1 (p.44)
chants, #5-40 (p.57), #5-44 (p.59), #8-3 (p.85)
Charades game #4-29 (p.39)
Chicken Smells Good, The #6-5 (p.63)
Christison, Mary Ann #1-11 (p.11), #4-4 (p.31), #4-13 (p.34)
Church, Mary Mitchell #6-9 (p.64)
Citizen Handbook #10-25 (p.116)
citizenship. *See* Chapter 10 (pp.112–116)
Citizenship Made Simple #10-14 (p.113)
Citizenship Now #10-15 (p.113)

Citizenship: Passing the Test #10-16 (p.113)
Claire, Elizabeth #4-31 (p.40), editor #6-19 (p.68), #9-16 (p.98), #11-11 (p.123)
Clark, Raymond C. #4-8 (p.32)
class management, #1-2 (p.8), #1-9 (p.10), #1-11 (p.11), #1-17 (p.12)
Clear Speech #5-38 (p.57)
Coelho, Elizabeth #5-8 (p.46)
Cohn, David #12-7 (p.130)
Collaborations series #2-1 (p.16), #3-9 (p.24)
collaborative instruction
    about, #1-11 (p.11)
    activities for, #1-11 (p.11)
    definition of, *see* Glossary under 'co-operative' (p.147)
Collin, P. H. #9-7 (p.95)
Collins COBUILD Learner's Dictionary #9-12 (p.97)
Comics and Conversation #4-23 (p.37)
Communication Starters #4-3 (p.30)
communicative instruction
    about, #1-3 (p.8), #1-7 (p.9), #1-12 (p.11), #1-23 (p.13)
    activities for, #2-3 (p.17), #2-4 (p.18), #3-15 (p.27), #3-18 (p.28), #4-1 (p.30), #4-2 (p.30), #4-3 (p.30), #4-4 (p.31), #4-5 (p.31), #4-6 (p.32), #4-9 (p.32), #4-10 (p.33), #4-14 (p.34), #4-16 (p.35), #4-18 (p.36), #4-22 (p.37), #5-4 (p.44), #5-6 (p.45), #5-8 (p.46), #8-4 (p.85), #8-5 (p.85), #10-6 (p.109), #10-7 (p.109), #10-11 (p.111)
    definition of, *see* Glossary (p.147)
    how to teach, #5-4 (p.44), #8-7 (p.86)
community
    about, #10-25 (p.116)
    student activities in, #5-11 (p.47), #11-5 (p.121), #11-13 (p.124)
    See also Chapter 11 (pp.124–126)
Community Spirit #1-11 (p.11)
competency-based instruction
    about, #3-3 (p.22), #3-8 (p.24)
    definition of, *see* Glossary (p.147)

examples of, #2-5 (p.19), #3-12 (p.26), #10-1 (p.106)

computer skills, #7-2 (p.76), #12-4 (p.129), #12-5 (p.129), #12-7 (p.130)

computer software, #8-10 (p.87), #8-11 (p.87), #8-16 (p.90), #9-4 (p.93), #9-8 (p.95), #9-9 (p.96), #9-11 (p.96), #9-15 (p.98), #13-3 (p.135), #13-8 (p.136)

Connect with English video series #12-2 (p.127)

Connelly, Michael #6-25 (p.70)

Contact USA #6-18 (p.67)

context-based instruction, #2-6 (p.20), #5-10 (p.46), #8-9 (p.86), #8-10 (p.87), #8-12 (p.88), #8-15 (p.89), #9-22 (p.101)

definition of, *see* Glossary (p.147)

conversation
activities for, #4-13 (p.34), #4-26 (p.38), #4-30 (p.39), #4-31 (p.40), #4-34 (p.40), #5-2 (p.44), #5-3 (p.44), #5-4 (p.44), #5-6 (p.45), #5-9 (p.46), #5-10 (p.46), #5-11 (p.47), #5-12 (p.47), #5-14 (p.48), #5-17 (p.49), #9-19 (p.100)
how to teach, #5-2 (p.44)
See also discussion; *see* Chapter 5 (pp.43–60)

Conversation #5-2 (p.44)

Conversation Book, A series #5-10 (p.46)

Conversation Inspirations #5-3 (p.44)

Conversations in English #2-2 (p.17)

cooperative learning
about, #1-7 (p.9)
definition of, *see* Glossary (p.147)
activities for, #5-8 (p.46), #7-2 (p.76)

coursebooks. See Chapter 2. *See also* under levels (beginning, intermediate, advanced, literacy, multilevel)

Crandall, JoAnn #2-4 (p.18), editor #3-3 (p.22)

Creative Questions #8-1 (p.84)

Crossroads Café video series #12-3 (p.128)

Crossroads series #2-3 (p.17)

Cuisenaire rods, use in language learning, #4-3 (p.30)

Culturally Speaking #5-11 (p.47)

culture
Canadian, #13-4 (p.135), #13-30 (p.143)
International, #7-8 (p.78), #11-12 (p.124), #13-4 (p.135), #13-18 (p.139)
U.S., #4-34 (p.40), #4-37 (p.42), #5-11 (p.47), #5-17 (p.49), #6-18 (p.67), #6-19 (p.68), #8-12 (p.88), #9-20 (p.100), #10-11 (p.111), #11-2 (p.120), #11-3 (p.120), #11-5 (p.121), #11-7 (p.122), #11-8 (p.123), #11-13 (p.124), #13-12 (p.137)
See also holidays

Cummings, Martha Graves #5-11 (p.47)

current events. *See* news stories

curriculum planning, #1-2 (p.8), #1-5 (p.9), #1-9 (p.10), #1-23 (p.13), #1-24 (p.13), #1-25 (p.14), #3-6 (p.23), #5-5 (p.45), #13-24 (p.141)

D

Dangerous English 2000! #9-16 (p.98)

Dave Sperling's Internet Guide #12-6 (p.130)

Dave's ESL Café website #12-8 (p.131)

Davidson, David M. #7-9 (p.79), #7-13 (p.81)

Davis, James E. #10-25 (p.116)

Davis, Paul #5-19 (p.50)

Davis, Sharryl #10-25 (p.116)

Day by Day #10-4 (p.108)

deaf students, #7-4 (p.77)

decision making. *See* problem solving

DeRocco, David #6-10 (p.65), #11-12 (p.124)

Designing Tasks for the Communicative Classroom #1-12 (p.11)

dialogue journals, #7-4 (p.77)

dialogues, as language models, #2-3 (p.17), #2-5 (p.19), #3-10 (p.25), #5-7 (p.45), #5-11 (p.47), #5-17 (p.49), #5-42 (p.58), #9-4 (p.93), #9-15 (p.98), #10-1 (p.106), #10-2 (p.107), #10-3 (p.107), #10-4 (p.108)

Diaz, Cathy Seitchik #5-9 (p.46)

dictation
  how to use, #5-19 (p.50)
  texts for, #3-15 (p.27), #4-7 (p.32),
    #5-26 (p.52), #7-7 (p.78)
  in citizenship exam, preparation for,
    #10-19 (p.114), #10-23 (p.116)
Dictation #5-19 (p.50)
dictionaries. *See* Chapter 9 (pp.91–98).
  See also bilingual materials
Diolata, Edna T. #3-18 (p.28)
discussion, #5-4 (p.44), #5-8 (p.46),
  #5-11 (p.47), #5-12 (p.47), #5-16
  (p.48), #5-18 (p.49), #5-30 (p.53),
  #5-32 (p.54), #5-33 (p.54), #6-4
  (p.63), #7-3 (p.77), #7-8 (p.78),
  #10-6 (p.109), #10-11 (p.111),
  #11-3 (p.120), #12-10 (p.131)
  See also conversation
Discussions A to Z #5-12 (p.47)
Discussions that Work #5-4 (p.44)
Draper, George #10-9 (p.110)
Drawing on Experience #7-6 (p.78)
Drawing Out #4-4 (p.31)
Duffy, John #3-11 (p.25)
Dumicich, John, editor #4-26 (p.38),
  #7-6 (p.78)
Dundas, Joan #11-12 (p.124)
Dunkel, Patricia #5-27 (p.52)

E

Easy English News #6-19 (p.68)
Easy True Stories #6-6 (p.64)
Easy Visuals for English Language Teachers #4-24 (p.38)
Edge, Julian #1-13 (p.11)
editing skills, #7-7 (p.78), #7-11 (p.80)
Edwards, Laurie #10-15 (p.113)
Elbaum, Sandra #8-12 (p.88)
E-mail for English Teaching #12-4 (p.129)
English ASAP series #3-10 (p.25), #10-5
  (p.108)
English at Home and on the Road #11-4
  (p.121)
English for Everyday Activities #9-18
  (p.99)
English through Citizenship series #10-17
  (p.114)
English through Citizenship: Game
  #10-18 (p.114)

error correction, #1-13 (p.11), #4-10
  (p.33), #7-1 (p.76), #7-11 (p.80),
  #8-4 (p.85)
ESL for Action #10-6 (p.109)
ESL Miscellany, The #9-20 (p.100)
ESL Starter Kit, The #1-2 (p.8)
ESL Teacher's Holiday Activities Kit
  #11-11 (p.123)
Even More True Stories #6-20 (p.68)
Everyday American English Dictionary
  #9-6 (p.94)
Everyday Idioms for Reference and Practice series #9-23 (p.102)
Eyring, Janet, article cited in #1-8
  (p.10)

F

Face to Face #11-5 (p.121)
Facts & Figures #6-7 (p.64)
Feare, Ronald E. #9-23 (p.102)
First Class Reader! #3-11 (p.25)
First Words in English #3-12 (p.26)
Firsten, Richard #8-15 (p.89)
Fischer, Sara #11-9 (p.123)
Five-Minute Activities #4-5 (p.31)
Focus on Grammar series #8-10 (p.87),
  #8-11 (p.87)
Focus on Speaking #5-5 (p.45)
Foley, Barbara H. #5-30 (p.53), #5-32
  (p.54), #8-14 (p.88), #10-1 (p.106)
folktales and traditional stories, #6-13
  (p.66), #6-24 (p.70), #7-8 (p.78),
  #13-7 (p.136)
For Your Information #6-21 (p.68)
Forest, T. #5-31 (p.54)
Fotinos, Sandra Douglas #5-10 (p.46)
four-skills approach. *See* integrated
  approach
Fragiadakis, Helen Kalkstein #5-7 (p.45),
  #9-22 (p.101)
Frankel, Irene #2-3 (p.17)
Frauman-Prickel, Maxine #4-21
  (p.37)
free materials, #1-2 (p.8), #3-8 (p.24),
  #4-28 (p.39), #4-29 (p.39), #10-20
  (p.115), #12-9 (p.131), #12-10
  (p.131), #12-11 (p.131), #12-12
  (p.132), #13-9 (p.137), #13-24
  (p.141). *See also* pp.125–126

free reading
  arguments for, #6-2 (p.63)
  See also pleasure reading
Freeman, Daniel B. #9-2 (p.92), #10-3
  (p.107)
From Writing to Composing #7-7 (p.78)
Fuchs, Marjorie #8-11 (p.87), #9-8
  (p.95)
functional approach
  definition of, *see* Glossary (p.147)
  texts using, #5-13 (p.47), #5-17
    (p.49), #5-44 (p.59), #10-4 (p.108)
Functions of American English #5-13
  (p.47)

G

games. *See* Chapter 4 (pp.39–40)
Games for Language Learning #4-6 (p.32)
Gardner, David, editor #4-17 (p.35)
Genser, Carol #5-1 (p.44)
Genzel, Rhona B. #5-11 (p.47)
Get Ready #5-39 (p.57)
Giannotti, Janet #11-7 (p.122)
Gilbert, Judy B. #5-38 (p.57)
Goldstein, Sharon #5-43 (p.58)
Gomez-Sanford, Rosario #1-25 (p.14)
Good News, Bad News #5-25 (p.52)
government, participation in, #10-13
  (p.112), #10-25 (p.116), #10-26
  (p.117)
Graham, Carolyn #5-40 (p.57), #5-44
  (p.59), #8-3 (p.85)
Gramer, Margot F. #9-1 (p.92)
grammar. *See* Chapter 8 (pp.83–90)
  See also questions; error correction;
    grammar practice; poetry
Grammar Book, The #8-2 (p.84)
Grammar Chants #8-3 (p.85)
Grammar Games #8-4 (p.85)
Grammar in Context series #8-12 (p.88)
grammar practice
  activities and exercises for, #4-3
    (p.30), #4-15 (p.35), #4-18 (p.36),
    #5-6 (p.45), #7-12 (p.80), #8-1
    (p.84), #8-4 (p.85), #8-5 (p.85),
    #8-7 (p.86), #8-9 (p.86), #8-13
    (p.88), #8-15 (p.89), #9-8 (p.95)
Grammar Practice Activities #8-5 (p.85)
GrammarWork series #8-13 (p.88)

Greenberg, Ingrid A. #5-16 (p.48)
Grenough, Millie #4-37 (p.42)
GRIDIT! #4-30 (p.39)
Grogan, Patricia E. #5-45 (p.59)
Grognet, Allene Guss #2-4 (p.18),
  #10-13 (p.112)
group projects. *See* collaborative instruc-
  tion; cooperative learning; small
  group work
Grundy, Peter #3-5 (p.23)
Guth, Gloria J. A. #3-6 (p.23)
Guy, Anne Marie #7-2 (p.76)

H

Hagen, Stacy A. #5-45 (p.59)
Haight, Michele #10-2 (p.107)
Haleem, Sofia #4-27 (p.39)
Hancock, Mark #5-37 (p.57)
Handbook for ESL Literacy, A #3-7
  (p.23)
Hands-on English #4-7 (p.32), #13-14
  (p.138)
Harmer, Jeremy #8-7 (p.86)
Hartmann, Pamela #6-27 (p.71)
Haverson, Wayne W. #3-1 (p.22)
Headstarts #6-1 (p.62)
Hemphill, David #10-11 (p.111)
Henderson, Sara Cook #5-41 (p.58)
Hess, Natalie #6-1 (p.62), #8-1 (p.84)
Heyer, Sandra #3-19 (p.28), #6-6
  (p.64), #6-14 (p.66), #6-20 (p.68)
Hilles, Sharon L. #8-8 (p.86)
Hirschy, Margaret W. #10-24 (p.116)
Hirschy, Patricia L. #10-24 (p.116)
history, U.S., #11-1 (p.119), #11-7
  (p.122), #11-11 (p.123)
  See also citizenship, Chapter 10
    (pp.105–117)
Hockman, Barbara #10-11 (p.111)
holidays, #4-34 (p.40), #7-13 (p.81),
  #8-9 (p.86), #11-8 (p.123), #11-9
  (p.123), #11-10 (p.123), #11-11
  (p.123), #11-12 (p.124)
Hughes, Arthur #1-19 (p.12)
Huizenga, Jann #2-1 (p.16), #5-31
  (p.54), #6-23 (p.69), #7-14
  (p.81)
humanistic instruction #1-10 (p.10)
Hyzer, Keesia Harrison #6-9 (p.64)

I

ice breakers. *See* warmups

idioms. See Chapter 9 (pp.101–103)

immigrant experience, #6-8 (p.64), #6-9 (p.64), #6-11 (p.65), #6-12 (p.65), #6-15 (p.66), #6-19 (p.68), #7-8 (p.78), #7-11 (p.80)

immigration, history of, #10-17 (p.114)

Improving Aural Comprehension #5-26 (p.52)

In Context #6-26 (p.70)

Index Card Games for ESL #4-8 (p.32)

individualized instruction. *See* self access

information gap technique, #4-2 (p.30), #4-15 (p.35), #5-8 (p.46), #13-11 (p.137)

Ingram, Beverly #7-7 (p.78)

Inness, Donna #4-15 (p.35)

INS (Immigration and Naturalization Service) website #10-20 (p.115)

INS Citizenship Interview: Will They Pass?, The #10-19 (p.114)

Insights for Today #6-22 (p.69)

integrated approach

about, #1-8 (p.10)

examples of, #2-1 (p.16), #2-2 (p.17), #2-3 (p.17), #2-4 (p.18), #3-4 (p.22), #3-9 (p.24), #3-10 (p.25), #3-11 (p.25), #3-12 (p.26), #3-13 (p.26), #3-18 (p.28), #5-7 (p.45), #7-3 (p.77), #8-10 (p.87), #8-14 (p.88), #9-24 (p.102), #10-5 (p.108), #10-8 (p.109), #10-10 (p.110), #11-4 (p.121), #11-5 (p.121), #11-7 (p.122), #12-2 (p.127), #12-3 (p.128)

Interactions One: A Reading Skills Book #6-27 (p.71)

interactive instruction

about, #1-3 (p.8), #1-21 (p.13)

definition of, *see* Glossary (p.147)

activities for, #1-5 (p.9), #1-11 (p.11), #1-21 (p.13), #4-12 (p.34), #6-1 (p.62)

See also communicative instruction; student-centered instruction

Interactive Techniques for the ESL Classroom #4-9 (p.32)

Interactive Tutorial, The #4-10 (p.33)

intermediate level

activities & exercises for, #4-9 (p.32), #4-15 (p.35), #4-16 (p.35), #4-30 (p.39), #4-31 (p.40), #5-3 (p.44), #5-4 (p.44), #5-8 (p.46), #5-37 (p.57), #6-1 (p.62), #7-3 (p.77), #7-5 (p.77), #7-6 (p.78), #8-3 (p.85), #8-15 (p.89)

description of, *see* Introduction (p.1)

pictures & picture stories for, #9-2 (p.92), #9-5 (p.94), #9-18 (p.99), #9-19 (p.100)

stories & readings for, #6-8 (p.64), #6-15 (p.66), #6-16 through #6-25 (pp.67-70), #12-10 (p.131)

texts & coursebooks for, #2-1 (p.16), #2-3 (p.17), #2-4 (p.18), #2-5 (p.19), #5-23 (p.51), #7-7 (p.78), #7-8 (p.78), #7-9 (p.79), #7-11 (p.80), #7-14 (p.81), #8-11 (p.87), #8-12 (p.88), #8-13 (p.88), #8-14 (p.88), #9-22 (p.101), #10-1 (p.106), #10-3 (p.107), #10-4 (p.108), #10-5 (p.108), #10-6 (p.109), #10-8 (p.109), #10-10 (p.110), #10-11 (p.111), #10-12 (p.111), #11-1 (p.119), #11-4 (p.121), #11-13 (p.124)

Intermediate Listening Comprehension #5-27 (p.52)

International Holiday & Festival Primer, The #11-12 (p.124)

internet

about, #12-6 (p.130)

activities for, #12-7 (p.130)

websites for ESL, #12-8 (p.131), #12-9 (p.131), #12-10 (p.131)

other online resources, #1-2 (p.8), #10-20 (p.115), #10-26 (p.117), #12-11 (p.131), #12-12 (p.132)

See also publishers' websites listed in Chapter 13 (p.133)

Internet Tasks for Second Language Students #12-7 (p.130)

intonation, #5-36 (p.56), #5-37 (p.57), #5-38 (p.57), #5-39 (p.57), #5-40 (p.57), #5-41 (p.58), #5-42 (p.58), #5-46 (p.59)

Introducing the USA #11-6 (p.122)
Isserlis, Janet #2-2 (p.17)

J

Jazz Chants #5-40 (p.57) *See also* chants
jigsaw technique. *See* information gap
Johnston, Susan S. #6-26 (p.70)
Jolly, Julia #11-2 (p.120)
Jones, Leo #5-13 (p.47)
journal writing, #7-8 (p.78)
    See also dialogue journals
Joyce, Helen #5-5 (p.45)
Just-A-Minute! #4-31 (p.40)

K

Kanter, Susan #8-15 (p.89)
Kasser, Carol #6-13 (p.66)
Kealey, James #4-15 (p.35)
Keep Talking #5-6 (p.45)
Kennedy, James H. #11-10 (p.123)
Keystrokes to Literacy #12-5 (p.129)
Kimmel, Barbara Brooks #10-14 (p.113)
King, Carol #7-7 (p.78)
Kirn, Elaine #6-27 (p.71), #10-17
    (p.114), #10-18 (p.114)
Klebanow, Barbara #11-9 (p.123)
Klippel, Friederike #5-6 (p.45)
Koch, Kamla Devi #3-14 (p.27)
Krashen, Stephen D. #1-14 (p.11), #6-2
    (p.63)

L

Lamb, Clarice #1-18 (p.12)
Language Experience approach, #1-6
    (p.9), #3-3 (p.22), #3-16 (p.27)
Laroy, Clement #5-36 (p.56)
Larsen-Freeman, Diane #8-2 (p.84)
Laubach Literacy Action #1-6 (p.9)
League of Women Voters website
    #10-26 (p.117)
learner centered teaching. *See* student
    centered instruction
Learner-Centered Curriculum, The #1-23
    (p.13)
Lee, Linda #7-8 (p.78)
lesson planning, #1-2 (p.8), #1-4 (p.8),
    #1-5 (p.9), #3-17 (p.27), #5-22
    (p.51), #8-8 (p.86)
Let's Work Safely #10-7 (p.109)

levels
    descriptions of, *see* Introduction (p.1)
    See also beginning, intermediate, ad-
        vanced, literacy, multilevel
Levine, Deena R. #11-3 (p.120)
Lexicarry #9-19 (p.100)
Liebowitz, Dorothy Gabel #9-17 (p.99)
Lifelines series #10-1 (p.106)
LifePrints series #2-4 (p.18), #10-21
    (p.115)
lifeskills. *See* survival skills
Ligon, Fred #5-15 (p.48)
Lim, Phyllis L. #5-27 (p.52)
Lindstromberg, Seth, editor #4-14
    (p.34), editor #4-16 (p.35)
Listen and Say It Right in English #5-14
    (p.48)
Listen First #5-28 (p.53)
Listen to Me! #5-30 (p.53)
listening. *See* Chapter 5 (pp.50–55)
    See also reduced forms
"Listening Comprehension in
    Second/Foreign Language Instruction"
    article #5-20 (p.50)
Listening in Action #5-21 (p.51)
*Listening Tasks for Intermediate Students
    of English* #5-29 (p.53)
literacy level
    activities & exercises for, #3-7 (p.23),
        #4-2 (p.30), #4-3 (p.30), #4-4
        (p.31), #4-8 (p.32), #4-11 (p.33),
        #4-21 (p.37), #4-22 (p.37),
        #4-28 (p.39), #5-24 (p.51),
        #5-40 (p.57)
    description of, *see* Introduction (p.1)
    how to teach, #1-8 (p.10), #3-1
        (p.22), #3-3 (p.22), #3-5 (p.23),
        #3-6 (p.23), #3-7 (p.23), #3-8
        (p.24), #3-16 (p.27), #5-1 (p.44)
    issues about, #3-2 (p.22), #3-7 (p.23)
    pictures & picture stories for, #3-19
        (p.28), #4-21 (p.37), #5-1 (p.44),
        #5-15 (p.48), #6-6 (p.64), #9-1
        (p.92)
    texts and coursebooks for, #2-3 (p.17),
        #2-5 (p.19), #3-4 (p.22), #3-9
        through #3-19 (pp.24-28), #9-1
        (p.92), #12-5 (p.129)
    See also Chapter 3 (pp.21–28)

Literacy Volunteers of New York #6-8 (p.64)

Little, Linda W. #5-16 (p.48)

Live Action English #4-11 (p.33)

Lockhart, Charles #1-15 (p.11)

Longman Dictionary of American English #9-8 (p.95)

Longman ESL Literacy #3-13 (p.26)

Longman Language Activator #9-14 (p.98)

Longman Photo Dictionary #9-2 (p.92)

Look Again Pictures #4-25 (p.38)

Lowi, Miriam #9-7 (p.95)

Lubiner, Alan M. #10-14 (p.113)

Lund, Andreas #12-9 (p.131)

M

Macdonald, Marion #4-1 (p.30)

Mackey, Daphne #5-39 (p.57), #6-18 (p.67)

Magy, Ronna #6-11 (p.65), #10-12 (p.111), #10-22 (p.115)

Making It Happen #1-3 (p.8)

Making Meaning, Making Change #1-24 (p.13)

maps
    teaching with, #4-3 (p.30), #4-27 (p.39), #10-17 (p.114), #10-24 (p.116), #11-1 (p.119), #11-14 (p.125)
    source for, #13-23 (p.141)

Mare, Nancy Nici #6-22 (p.69)

math skills
    integrated into class work, #3-9 (p.24), #10-10 (p.110), #11-14 (p.125)
    source for books on, #13-37 (p.145)

May I Help You? #10-8 (p.109)

McGrail, Loren #1-25 (p.14)

McKay, Heather #1-5 (p.9), #4-22 (p.37), #7-3 (p.77), #7-5 (p.77)

McKay, Irene S. #8-9 (p.86)

McKay, Sandra L. #3-2 (p.22)

McPartland, Pamela #9-24 (p.102)

Mentel, James #2-6 (p.20)

methods. *See* Chapter 1 (pp.7–14). *See also* under specific teaching methods and approaches

Meyers, Cliff #2-3 (p.17)

Miller, Lindsay, editor #4-17 (p.35)

minimal pairs, #5-35 (p.56), #5-41 (p.58)

mistakes. *See* error correction

Mistakes and Correction #1-13 (p.11)

Molinsky, Steven J. #10-4 (p.108), #10-23 (p.116)

Mollica, Anthony #4-20 (p.36)

Moore, Douglas E. #12-7 (p.130)

Moran, Patrick R. #9-19 (p.100)

Morgan, John #9-21 (p.100)

Morley, Joan #5-20 (p.50), #5-26 (p.52)

Moskowitz, Gertrude #1-10 (p.10)

Moss, Donna #3-9 (p.24)

Mosteller, Lee #10-2 (p.107)

Moving On #5-31 (p.54)

Mrowicki, Linda #2-2 (p.17), #3-12 (p.26), #3-14 (p.27), #3-15 (p.27), #3-17 (p.27), #10-7 (p.109)

Multicultural Workshop, The #7-8 (p.78)

multilevel classes
    activities suitable for, #1-9 (p.10), #1-11 (p.11), #4-7 (p.32), #4-17 (p.35), #4-20 (p.36), #4-26 (p.38), #5-8 (p.46), #5-9 (p.46), #5-40 (p.57), #11-13 (p.124)
    how to teach, #1-2 (p.8), #1-9 (p.10), #1-17 (p.12), #3-17 (p.27)
    texts suitable for, #2-3 (p.17), #2-5 (p.19), #3-9 (p.24), #6-11 (p.65), #6-13 (p.66), #10-10 (p.110)

Murphy, Peter #11-6 (p.122)

music, #4-37 (p.42)

My Native Land #6-8 (p.64)

N

Nash, Andrea #1-25 (p.14)

Neblett, Elizabeth R. #8-14 (p.88)

needs assessment. *See* assessment

Nelson, Gayle #4-12 (p.34)

New Beginning, A #6-9 (p.64)

New Grammar in Action, The #8-14 (p.88)

New Oxford Picture Dictionary CD-ROM, The #9-4 (p.93)

New Oxford Picture Dictionary, The #9-3 (p.93)

new teachers, #1-2 (p.8), #1-4 (p.8), #1-5 (p.9), #1-6 (p.9), #1-8 (p.10),

#3-11 (p.25), #4-1 (p.30), #4-5 (p.31), #6-12 (p.65)
Newbury House Dictionary of American English, The #9-9 (p.96)
Newman, Christy M. #2-4 (p.18), #10-21 (p.115)
news stories
    human interest readings about, #3-19 (p.28), #5-25 (p.52), #6-4 (p.63), #6-6 (p.64), #6-14 (p.66), #6-16 (p.67), #6-19 (p.68), #6-20 (p.68), #6-21 (p.68), #6-23 (p.69)
    human interest listening, #5-32 (p.54), #5-33 (p.54)
    See also nonfiction stories
newspapers
    for ESL, #6-19 (p.68), #13-26 (p.142)
    international, #12-11 (p.131)
    teaching with, #11-14 (p.125)
Niedermeier, Ann Marie #6-9 (p.64)
NIFL-ESL online forum #12-12 (p.132)
Nilsen, Alleen Pace #5-35 (p.56)
Nilsen, Don L. F. #5-35 (p.56)
Nishio, Yvonne Wong #3-13 (p.26)
Nolasco, Rob #5-2 (p.44)
nonfiction stories
    readings, #6-7 (p.64), #6-10 (p.65), #6-18 (p.67), #6-22 (p.69), #6-25 (p.70), #6-26 (p.70), #6-27 (p.71), #8-12 (p.88), #12-10 (p.131)
    listening, #5-27 (p.52), #6-7 (p.64)
    See also news stories
Now Hear This! #5-32 (p.54)
NTC's American English Learner's Dictionary #9-13 (p.97)
numbers, practice with, #3-5 (p.23), #3-15 (p.27), #4-28 (p.39), #5-24 (p.51), 5-26 (p.52)
    See also math skills
Nunan, David #1-12 (p.11), #1-18 (p.12), #1-23 (p.13)

O

Olsen, Judy Winn-Bell #4-2 (p.30), #4-3 (p.30), #4-25 (p.38), #5-8 (p.46)
On the Air #5-33 (p.54)
Operations in English #4-12 (p.34)
Orion, Gertrude F. #5-42 (p.58)

Oxford American Wordpower Dictionary #9-11 (p.96)
Oxford Picture Dictionary, The #9-5 (p.94)

P

pairwork, #3-15 (p.27), #3-18 (p.28), #4-2 (p.30), #4-5 (p.31), #4-10 (p.33), #5-6 (p.45), #5-43 (p.58)
Palmer, Adrian S. #4-2 (p.30)
Parnwell, E.C. #9-3 (p.93)
participatory approach
    about, #1-24 (p.13), #1-25 (p.14), #3-3 (p.22)
    See also problem posing
Partnerships in Learning: Teaching ESL to Adults #1-4 (p.8)
PD's: Pronunciation Drills in Depth #5-41 (p.58)
Penn, Norgina Wright #6-17 (p.67)
People at Work #10-9 (p.110)
performance-based instruction, #3-8 (p.24)
    definition of, *see* Glossary (p.147)
Personal Stories #3-14 (p.27)
Peters, Sandy and Thomas #12-10 (p.131)
Peyton, Joy Kreeft, editor #3-3 (p.22), editor #7-4 (p.77)
Pfaffenberger, Barbara #10-11 (p.111)
Pickett, William P. #6-5 (p.63)
Pictionary game #4-32 (p.40)
Picture is Worth . . . 1000 Words, A #4-20 (p.36)
Picture It! #4-26 (p.38)
picture stories, #3-9 (p.24), #3-18 (p.28), #3-19 (p.28), #4-21 (p.37), #4-23 (p.37), #4-26 (p.38), #5-1 (p.44), #5-15 (p.48), #5-30 (p.53), #6-6 (p.64), #10-3 (p.107), #11-11 (p.123)
    See also under each level; visuals
Picture Stories #5-15 (p.48)
pictures. *See* visuals
Pike-Baky, Meredith #7-10 (p.79)
pleasure reading
    description of, *see* Chapter 6 (p.61)
poetry, grammar and, #12-9 (p.131)
Pollard, Laurel #8-1 (p.84)

Pomann, Howard #10-1 (p.106)
Power of Reading, The #6-2 (p.63)
Powerhouse Publishing, #10-19
  (p.114)
Practical English Usage #8-6 (p.85)
Practice with Your Partner #3-15 (p.27)
pre-reading activities, #6-1 (p.62), #6-6
  (p.64), #6-7 (p.64), 6-15 (p.66)
pre-writing activities, #4-4 (p.31),
  #4-20 (p.36), #7-3 (p.77), #7-5
  (p.77), #7-13 (p.81)
*Principles and Practice in Second Lan-
  guage Acquisition* #1-14 (p.11)
problem-posing approach
  examples of, #7-4 (p.77), #10-6
    (p.109)
  definition of, *see* Glossary (p.147)
problem solving, #1-5 (p.9), #4-9 (p.32),
  #4-15 (p.35), #5-16 (p.48), #5-18
  (p.49)
Problem Solving #5-16 (p.48)
process writing, #7-1 (p.76), #7-2 (p.76),
  #7-6 (p.78), #7-7 (p.78), #7-10
  (p.79), #7-11 (p.80)
program management. *See* class
  management
Pronouncing American English #5-42
  (p.58)
pronunciation
  about, #5-35 (p.56)
  activities and exercises for, #5-42
    (p.58), #5-44 (p.59), #8-3 (p.85)
  games for, #5-37 (p.57)
  See also Chapter 5 (pp.56–60)
Pronunciation #5-36 (p.56)
Pronunciation Contrasts in English #5-35
  (p.56)
Pronunciation Games #5-37 (p.57)
Pronunciation Pairs #5-43 (p.58)
Purple Cows and Potato Chips #4-13
  (p.34)
Put It in Writing #7-9 (p.79)
puzzles, #4-7 (p.32), #4-9 (p.32), #4-10
  (p.33), #4-33 (p.40), #4-35 (p.41),
  #4-36 (p.41), #13-14 (p.138)

Q

Quatrini, Susan C. #10-10 (p.110)
questions, #8-1 (p.84)

R

Raimes, Ann #7-1 (p.76)
*Random House Webster's Basic Dictio-
  nary of American English* #9-10 (p.96)
Reader's Choice #6-28 (p.71)
reading. *See* Chapter 6 (pp.61–73).
  See also news stories; pre-reading
  activities; scanning; literacy; nonfiction stories. *See also under each
  level* (literacy, beginning, intermediate, advanced, multilevel).
reading theory, #6-2 (p.63)
Reading Workout #6-23 (p.69)
Real-Life English Grammar series #8-15
  (p.89)
Real-Life English series #2-5 (p.19)
real-life topics. *See* survival skills
Recipe Book, The #4-14 (p.34)
reduced forms, in speech, #5-34 (p.55)
reference. *See* teacher reference
Reflection and Beyond #7-10 (p.79)
*Reflective Teaching in Second Language
  Classrooms* #1-15 (p.11)
register, #5-14 (p.48), #5-17 (p.49)
retelling, #5-1 (p.44), #6-4 (p.63),
  #6-13 (p.66)
  See also story telling
Rhum, Madeline #1-25 (p.14)
rhythm, in speech, #5-36 (p.56), #5-37
  (p.57), #5-38 (p.57), #5-40 (p.57),
  #5-44 (p.59)
Richard-Amato, Patricia A. #1-3 (p.8)
Richards, Jack C. #1-1 (p.8), #1-15
  (p.11), #5-23 (p.51)
Rideout, Philip M. #9-9 (p.96)
Ringel, Harry #6-15 (p.66)
Rinvolucri, Mario #5-19 (p.50), #8-4
  (p.85) #9-21 (p.100)
Robinson, Julia #1-4 (p.8)
Rodgers, Carol Richardson #5-15 (p.48)
Rodgers, Theodore S. #1-1 (p.8), #4-2
  (p.30)
Rogers-Gordon, Sue #4-1 (p.30)
role of teachers and learners, #1-1 (p.8),
  #1-16 (p.12)
roleplay, #4-9 (p.32), #4-14 (p.34), #5-3
  (p.44), #5-4 (p.44), #5-11 (p.47),
  #5-13 (p.47), #5-17 (p.49), #7-5
  (p.77), #10-7 (p.109), #10-8 (p.109)

Roles of Teachers and Learners #1-16 (p.12)
Romijn, Elizabeth #4-11 (p.33)
Romo, Richard #4-24 (p.38)
Rooks, George M. #7-11 (p.80)
Root, Christine #6-21 (p.68), #7-6 (p.78)
Rosenthal, Marilyn S. #9-2 (p.92)
Rost, Michael #5-21 (p.51)
Ruttenberg, Arlene #3-14 (p.27)

S

Sadow, Catherine #5-33 (p.54), #10-9 (p.110)
Sanders, Karen M. #4-10 (p.33)
Sather, Edgar #5-33 (p.54)
Sathow, Edgar #10-9 (p.110)
Savage, K. Lynn, editor #12-3 (p.128)
Scane, Joyce #7-2 (p.76)
scanning, #6-25 (p.70)
SCANS-based instruction
    about, #13-9 (p.137)
    definition of, *see* Glossary (p.147)
    materials based on, #3-10 (p.25), #10-5 (p.108)
Schecter, Sandra R. #5-29 (p.53)
Schoenberg, Irene E. #4-34 (p.40), #5-18 (p.49), #8-10 (p.87)
Schwartz, Eileen A. #4-30 (p.39)
science topics, #6-25 (p.70)
Scrabble game #4-33 (p.40)
second language acquisition, theory of, #1-14 (p.11)
Seely, Contee #4-11 (p.33)
self access, #1-17 (p.12), #4-17 (p.35), #4-35 (p.41), #4-36 (p.41), #5-42 (p.58), #5-43 (p.58), #12-3 (p.128)
Self-Access #1-17 (p.12)
Self-Directed Teacher, The #1-18 (p.12)
Selman, Mary #1-4 (p.8)
sensory activities, #4-13 (p.34), #5-36 (p.56)
sequences, text-based, #4-11 (p.33), #4-12 (p.34)
    See also picture stories
Seufert-Bosco, Margaret #10-13 (p.112)
Shank, Cathy C. #3-9 (p.24)
Shapiro, Norma #5-1 (p.44), #9-5 (p.94)
Share Your Paragraph #7-11 (p.80)

Sheerin, Susan #1-17 (p.12)
Shenanigames #4-15 (p.35)
Shoemaker, Connie L. #4-9 (p.32)
Shoemaker, F. Floyd #4-9 (p.32)
Short Cuts series #2-6 (p.20)
Short, Deborah J. #10-13 (p.112)
Silberstein, Sandra #6-3 (p.63)
Silliman, Anna, editor #4-7 (p.32)
Silverman, Ann #6-13 (p.66)
Sims, Jean #6-25 (p.70)
simulation activities, #4-9 (p.32)
    See also roleplay
Sing it! series #4-37 (p.42)
situation based instruction. *See* context-based instruction
slang, #9-15 (p.98), #9-16 (p.98), #13-27 (p.142)
small group work, #1-11 (p.11), #2-6 (p.20), #4-1 (p.30), #4-8 (p.32), #4-30 (p.39), #4-31 (p.40), #5-6 (p.45), #7-3 (p.77)
    See also cooperative learning; information gap; roleplay
Small Talk #5-44 (p.59)
Smith, Jeanne H. #6-15 (p.66)
Smith, Lorraine C. #6-22 (p.69)
Solo, Duo, Trio #4-35 (p.41)
Sound Advantage #5-45 (p.59)
Sounds Great #5-46 (p.59)
Spanish language materials, #9-1 (p.92), #9-2 (p.92), #9-3 (p.93), #9-5 (p.94), #10-24 (p.116), #11-1 (p.119), #13-2 (p.134), #13-4 (p.135), #13-20 (p.140), #13-23 (p.141), #13-25 (p.141)
    See also bilingual materials
speaking. *See* Chapter 5 (pp.43–60)
    See also conversation; discussion; pronunciation
Speaking of Survival #10-3 (p.107)
Speaking Naturally #5-17 (p.49)
Spears, Richard A., editor #9-6 (p.94), editor #9-13 (p.97)
Sperling, Dave #12-6 (p.130), #12-8 (p.131)
Stack, Lydia #4-18 (p.36)
staff development. *See* teacher development
Stafford-Yilmaz, Lynn #11-13 (p.124)

Standby Book, The #4-16 (p.35)

Starkey, Carolyn Morton #6-17 (p.67)

Start Right #3-16 (p.27)

Starting to Read #3-17 (p.27)

Staton, Jana, editor #7-4 (p.77)

Stempleski, Susan, editor #12-1 (p.127)

Stevick, Earl W. #1-20 (p.12)

Stone, Antonia #12-5 (p.129)

Stories for the New Millennium #6-10 (p.65)

Stories from the Heart #6-11 (p.65)

Stories to Tell Our Children #6-12 (p.65)

Stories We Brought With Us #6-13 (p.66)

story telling, #4-14 (p.34), #4-20 (p.36), #4-23 (p.37), #4-26 (p.38), #5-1 (p.44), #5-15 (p.48), #7-9 (p.79), #7-13 (p.81)

See also retelling

Street Talk series #9-15 (p.98)

stress in speech, #5-36 (p.56), #5-37 (p.57), #5-38 (p.57), #5-39 (p.57), #5-40 (p.57), #5-42 (p.58), #5-44 (p.59), #5-46 (p.59)

student-centered instruction, #1-10 (p.10), #1-11 (p.11), #1-23 (p.13), #1-24 (p.13), #1-25 (p.14), #3-18 (p.28), #5-1 (p.44), #5-36 (p.56)

definition of, *see* Glossary (p.147)

student stories, #2-1 (p.16), #3-9 (p.24), #3-14 (p.27), #6-8 (p.64), #6-11 (p.65), #6-12 (p.65), #6-15 (p.66), #6-19 (p.68), #6-23 (p.69), #7-8 (p.78), #10-12 (p.111), #12-10 (p.131)

substitute teacher, lessons for, #4-4 (p.31), #4-5 (p.31), #4-20 (p.36), #4-37 (p.42), #5-3 (p.44), #5-15 (p.48), #5-19 (p.50), #5-24 (p.51), #7-13 (p.81)

Sudlow, Michael #11-4 (p.121)

Survival English series #10-2 (p.107)

survival skills, #2-5 (p.19), #3-4 (p.22), #3-12 (p.26), #3-13 (p.26), #4-25 (p.38), #6-17 (p.67), #9-18 (p.99), #10-1 (p.106), #10-2 (p.107), #10-3 (p.107), #11-4 (p.121)

Swan, Michael #8-6 (p.85)

*Szwarcewicz, Suzanne Mele #11-7 (p.122)

T

Takahashi, Noriko #4-21 (p.37)

Take Charge! #3-18 (p.28)

Take It Easy #9-24 (p.102)

Tales from Around the World #6-24 (p.70)

Taliercio-Cohn, Carmela #12-7 (p.130)

Talk About Trivia #4-34 (p.40)

Talk About Values #5-18 (p.49)

Talking About the U.S.A. #11-7 (p.122)

Talking Shop #1-25 (p.14)

Tannenbaum, Elizabeth #5-15 (p.48)

Tasks for Independent Language Learning #4-17 (p.35)

teacher development

self-analysis, #1-15 (p.11), #1-16 (p.12), #1-18 (p.12), #1-20 (p.12), #3-6 (p.23)

training and staff development, #1-24 (p.13)

teacher reference

culture, #11-3 (p.120), #11-8 (p.123)

dictionary, #9-14 (p.98)

grammar, #8-2 (p.84), #8-6 (p.85), #8-16 (p.90)

methods bibliography, #1-1 (p.8), #3-3 (p.22)

professional issues, #12-12 (p.132)

pronunciation, #5-35 (p.56), #5-41 (p.58), #5-45 (p.59)

vocabulary, #9-20 (p.100), #9-23 (p.102)

See also internet, online resources

teacher training. *See* teacher development

Teaching Adult Second Language Learners #1-5 (p.9)

Teaching Adults; An ESL Resource Book #1-6 (p.9)

Teaching and Learning Grammar #8-7 (p.86)

Teaching by Principles #1-7 (p.9)

Teaching English as a Second or Foreign Language #1-8 (p.10)

Teaching Listening Comprehension #5-22 (p.51)

teaching methods. *See* Chapter 1 (pp.7–14) *See also* under specific methods and approaches

Teaching Multilevel Classes in ESL #1-9 (p.10)

techniques, teaching. *See* chants; class management; dialogue journals; dialogues; dictation; information gap; Language Experience; pairwork, retelling; role play; self access; small group work; story telling; TPR; warmups

Techniques and Resources in Teaching Grammar #8-8 (p.86)

Techniques and Resources in Teaching Reading #6-3 (p.63)

Techniques for Classroom Interaction #1-21 (p.13)

Techniques in Teaching Writing #7-1 (p.76)

technology. *See* computer skills; computer software; internet; video

Templin, Elizabeth E. #6-26 (p.70)

Templin-Imel, Garnet #3-4 (p.22)

Terrill, Lynda #3-9 (p.24)

test-taking practice, #3-13 (p.26)

testing. *See* assessment

Testing for Language Teachers #1-19 (p.12)

Testing Spoken Language #1-22 (p.13)

Thematic Activities for Beginners in English #4-36 (p.41)

Thibaudeau, Sandra #6-4 (p.63), #6-16 (p.67)

Think, Write, Share #7-2 (p.76)

Thomas-Ruzic, Maria #6-23 (p.69), #7-14 (p.81)

Tiersky, Ethel #11-8 (p.123)

Tiersky, Martin #11-8 (p.123)

Tillitt, Bruce #5-17 (p.49)

Time and Space #6-25 (p.70)

TOEFL preparation, #5-45 (p.59), #8-16 (p.90)

Tom, Abigail #1-5 (p.9), #4-22 (p.37), #7-3 (p.77), #7-5 (p.77)

TOPICS Magazine, online #12-10 (p.131)

TPR (Total Physical Response) technique, #1-6 (p.9), #3-13 (p.26), #3-16 (p.27), #4-11 (p.33), #4-12 (p.34), #4-15 (p.35), #4-21 (p.37)

traditional stories. *See* folktales

Trager, Edith Crowell #5-41 (p.58)

True Stories series, #3-19 (p.28), #6-6 (p.64), #6-14 (p.66), #6-20 (p.68)

True Stories in the News #6-14 (p.66)

tutoring
  activities for, #1-6 (p.9), #4-3 (p.30), #4-7 (p.32), #4-8 (p.32), #4-10 (p.33), #4-17 (p.35)
  advanced students, #6-27 (p.71)
  materials for, #3-12 (p.26), #3-13 (p.26), #3-14 (p.27), #3-17 (p.27), #4-21 (p.37), #6-11 (p.65), #12-3 (p.128), #12-5 (p.129)
  resources for, #13-9 (p.137), #13-14 (p.138), #13-20 (p.140), #13-21 (p.140), #13-26 (p.142), #13-32 (p.143)
  tips on, #1-6 (p.9), #13-9 (p.137)

U

U.S. Citizen, Yes #10-22 (p.115)

U.S.A.: Customs and Institutions, The #11-8 (p.123)

Ultimate Collection of News Links website #12-11 (p.131)

Underhill, Nic #1-22 (p.13)

Understanding and Using English Grammar #8-16 (p.90)

United States culture. *See* culture

Ur, Penny #4-5 (p.31), #5-4 (p.44), #5-22 (p.51), #8-5 (p.85)

Urbom, Ruth, editor #9-11 (p.96)

Using the Newspaper to Teach Basic Living Skills #11-14 (p.125)

V

Van Ormer, Kathy S. #10-10 (p.110)

Very Easy True Stories #3-19 (p.28)

video
  about using, #3-6 (p.23), #12-1 (p.127)
  materials, #6-7 (p.64), #9-25 (p.103), #10-19 (p.114), #12-2 (p.127), #12-3 (p.128), #13-4 (p.135), #13-18 (p.139)

Video in Second Language Teaching #12-1 (p.127)

VIDIOMS #9-25 (p.103)

Virginia Adult Education and Literacy Centers #1-2 (p.8)

visuals
  how to create, #4-19 (p.36), #4-27 (p.39), #5-1 (p.44)

how to teach with, #4-24 (p.38)

ready-to-use drawings, #2-6 (p.20), #4-2 (p.30), #4-19 (p.36), #4-22 (p.37), #4-23 (p.37), #4-25 (p.38), #5-1 (p.44), #5-10 (p.46), #8-5 (p.85), #9-1 (p.92), #9-3 (p.93), #9-5 (p.94), #9-17 (p.99), #9-19 (p.100)

ready-to-use photos, #4-20 (p.36), #9-2 (p.92)

student-made, #4-4 (p.31), #7-6 (p.78)

See also picture stories

Visuals for the Language Classroom #4-27 (p.39)

vocabulary. *See* Chapter 9 (pp.91–101)

Vocabulary #9-21 (p.100)

Voices of Freedom #10-23 (p.116)

Von Baeyer, C. #5-13 (p.47)

W

Walker, Joanie #3-16 (p.27)

Wallerstein, Nina #10-6 (p.109)

Wallwork, Adrian #5-12 (p.47)

warmups, #1-10 (p.10), #4-2 (p.30), #4-5 (p.31), #4-13 (p.34), #4-14 (p.34), #4-18 (p.36), #4-31 (p.40), #5-9 (p.46), #5-40 (p.57), #7-5 (p.77)

Warschauer, Mark #12-4 (p.129)

Way to U.S. Citizenship, The #10-24 (p.116)

websites. *See* internet

Weiland, Carol #9-7 (p.95)

Weinstein, Nina #5-14 (p.48), #5-34 (p.55)

Weinstein-Shr, Gail #2-1 (p.16), #6-12 (p.65)

Weintraub, Lynne #10-16 (p.113)

Wenstrom, Lauren #7-2 (p.76)

Westheimer, Miriam #8-11 (p.87)

Whaddaya Say? #5-34 (p.55)

"What Non-Readers or Beginning Readers Need to Know," article #3-8 (p.24)

whole language instruction, #1-7 (p.9), #3-3 (p.22), #4-4 (p.31), #6-24 (p.70)

definition of, *see* Glossary (p.147)

Winer, Lise #5-8 (p.46)

Winters, Thomas #4-12 (p.34)

Withrow, Jean #7-12 (p.80)

Word Ways Cubes #4-18 (p.36)

Working Culture, The series #10-11 (p.111)

Working Experience, The series #6-15 (p.66)

Working It Out #10-12 (p.111)

Working with Teaching Methods #1-20 (p.12)

workplace instruction. *See* Chapter 10 (pp.108–111)

Workskills series #10-10 (p.110)

Wright, Andrew #4-5 (p.31), #4-6 (p.32), #4-19 (p.36), #4-27 (p.39)

Wright, Tony #1-16 (p.12)

Wrigley, Heide Spruck #3-6 (p.23), #10-8 (p.109)

Write After #7-3 (p.77)

Write from the Start #7-13 (p.81)

writing. *See* Chapter 7 (pp.75–82)

See also dialog journals; process writing; pre-writing; dictation

Writing Our Lives #7-4 (p.77)

Writing Warmups #7-5 (p.77)

Writing Workout #7-14 (p.81)

Y

Yorkey, Richard #4-35 (p.41)

Z

Zanger, Virginia Vogel #11-5 (p.121)

Zelman, Nancy Ellen #5-3 (p.44)

Zimmerman, Ian #11-12 (p.124)

Zukowski/Faust, Jean #6-26 (p.70)

Zwier, Lawrence J. #9-18 (p.99)